THE CHRIST

THE CHRISTIAN'S HIGH CALLING

Maurice Roberts

THE BANNER OF TRUTH TRUST

THE BANNER OF TRUTH TRUST
3 Murrayfield Road, Edinburgh EH12 6EL
P.O. Box 621, Carlisle, PA 17013, USA

✳

© Maurice Roberts 2000
First Published 2000
ISBN 0 85151 792 7

✳

Typeset in 11¹/₂/13pt Adobe Garamond at
The Banner of Truth Trust
Printed and bound in Great Britain by
Creative Print and Design (Wales)
Ebbw Vale

TO MY CONGREGATION
WITH DEEP APPRECIATION
FOR THEIR PRAYERS AND
KINDNESS

Publishers' Preface

As with the earlier title by the same author, *The Thought of God*, all the articles in this book originally appeared in *The Banner of Truth*, the magazine which Maurice Roberts has edited since January 1988. The thirty-one articles in this new collection all relate to the nature of the Christian life, seen as a high and heavenly calling: its conflicts and victories, its goal in the glory to come, and the need for faithfulness now if the 'salt' which Christ has brought into the midst of a fallen and corrupted world is not to 'lose its savour'.

The Publishers believe that there is indeed a savour of spiritual and heavenly realities in these articles. Like the earlier collection, *The Christian's High Calling* will help the reader to glimpse the greatness and glory of the God who has called his people to himself and to see with greater clarity the unspeakable privilege of possessing so high a destiny.

Contents

III The Christian's Enjoyment of Grace and Glory

IV Faithfulness in the Modern Church

THE NATURE OF THE
CHRISTIAN LIFE

1

'Where No Vision Is . . .'

Modern society has everything to live with and nothing to live for. Touch a button and we talk to friends all over the world. Australia and Hong Kong are as close to London by phone as Clacton-on-Sea. Touch another button and the man with a big enough aerial can watch the television programmes shown in New York or Honolulu. Press a switch and your letter goes by fax right across the world in less time than it takes to read it. The shops bulge with every commodity imaginable to make life easy and pleasant.

The strange fact is however that life is far from easy or pleasant for modern society. Something more than fast foods and fast pleasures is essential if society is to find happiness. Man's machines mock him. When he has mastered the skills necessary to manipulate computers and word processors the old boredom returns. An instinct deep down in man tells him that there is a 'something' which he needs to find and which all his modern appliances cannot supply.

Society, if we are not mistaken, is in a perishing state in spite of all the political rhetoric to the contrary. In communities where marriage and morality are becoming ever rarer; where people scarcely read and scarcely think; where pleasures are snatched at random to relieve the monotony and drudgery of life; where real love, or parenthood, or hope, or religion are virtually non-existent – in such communities it can scarcely be said that people *live*. Even the educated of our modern world seem content to remain, so far as eternal things are concerned, in a permanently vegetative state.

Modern society is perishing at a great rate. Stand on the street corner of any town; read any newspaper; speak to any typical citizen and the fearful thought comes home to the heart of any spiritual person: 'I live in a valley of death. The people who are moving about all around us are dead while they live. Modern society is living in a fool's paradise.'

Well does Solomon tell us that 'Where no vision is the people perish' (*Prov.* 29:18). The plight of modern society is diagnosed correctly in that one brief sentence. People are sadly visionless. They do not have any ideals to excite them. Consequently there is nothing to fight for, nothing to aim at, nothing to lift the heart to inspired effort or heroic self-sacrifice. Life has become devoid of purpose because it has become devoid of meaning. The word processor and the television cannot tell man what he needs to know as matters of first importance: Why am I here? Who put me here? Who is He? What does He want me to be and to do? What is to happen to me at last?

The history of our world over the past century and more is a record of vision-breakers who have smashed the vision which our civilisation was earlier based on. Charles Darwin was one of the pioneers. He stood in the forefront of a movement to overthrow the great vision of a God as the Creator of all things and ruler over all things in wisdom, power and love. Darwin was followed by men like Herbert Spencer and Thomas Huxley who had no faith in anything that God has said but who, along with a host of like-minded agnostics and humanists, worked to replace 'the heavenly vision' which our fathers before had had by a this-worldly materialism.

But the popular Victorian illusion of an ever-improving humanity was shattered by the grim realities of the First World War. The humanist's vision of a tomorrow made better, not by God but by impersonal forces of 'Nature', received a fatal blow when our war-wounded men returned from the trenches and told stories of mud, machine guns and massacre on the battle lines of Northern France. Then came the bleak age of the 'Modern Poets'. They were our century's heralds of a visionless pessimism. Whilst retaining the secular mind of the Victorian humanists they added to the humanist dream the dark colours of despair: 'Why go to church to worship a God who allows men to die in a sea of mud and bullets?'

By the 1920s and '30s, people were voting with their feet against the religion of their fathers: 'God has let us down. The scholars no longer believe in the Bible which our fathers lived by. To go to church is to perpetuate the delusion of an ignorant antiquity.'

By the '40s and '50s of this century the churches were beginning to feel the effects of this widespread drift away from the gospel. Christianity, so it was being popularly portrayed, was outdated. The vision of God and His gospel was becoming dim everywhere. Hollywood did very well out of it. It was the age of the cinema. Faithful souls still clung to the Bible but the masses were going in a different direction.

The generation which lived through the Second War made up its mind that '*their* children were going to have good things'. This meant a good education and also more money, freedom and happiness than had been known by earlier generations this century. As a result the rising post-war youth was well catered for in material things. Generally speaking, people now 'had never had it so good'. But material affluence left this maturing generation low in moral and spiritual understanding. By the 1960s the old morality, remnant of an earlier Protestant heritage, crumbled under the pressure extended by human lust to enjoy the baser passions of which men were before rightly ashamed.

The 1960s witnessed a quantum leap from decency to decadence in the moral realm. The West passed through a veritable paradigm shift in its ethical outlook. The rights of God over the consciences of men were now unashamedly rejected. In their place it was being openly asserted that it is *man* who has all the rights. This was the crossover point. A 'new morality' was emerging on all sides. Men have their *rights*, it was said. Women, too, discovered they had *rights*.

It was the age of nostalgic popular music. The artists were young and had no time for Jesus Christ – and were not afraid to say so. Those who believed in God or who followed the old standards were 'square', presumably misfits in this brave new and amoral world. It was felt to be wonderful to be alive (provided you were young and could enjoy the new freedom which was breaking down all the old barriers). There was now no crime except to be old-fashioned and sourly moral. Everyone who was anyone drank, danced and tried drugs.

But sin (not at the time a popular term for this new lifestyle) is a monster lying at the door. No sooner does man abandon the way of God than he becomes the tragic victim of his own newly-invented pleasures. Unheard of disease now struck our race. Those who play with fire must burn their fingers. So it came to pass at the very moment when anything and everything was to be an orgy of pleasure that our sad visionless society found that pleasure sought in the wrong way is a scorpion whose sting is in its tail. All the combined resources of rich nations could find no remedy for an insidious new form of death which reduced a strong and healthy young man to a living shadow, vulnerable to every passing virus. The vision of unlimited pleasure was proving to end in nightmare.

It is beyond our powers to know whether our sad, visionless and deeply lost society is to sink still farther into the morass before it cries to God for help. We fervently hope that it will not sink lower. Should God's hand permit society to slide still farther away from the light and truth of the Bible into yet deeper darkness, we shudder to imagine what manner of society it will become.

What we see and know to be happening all around us is grief enough to Christian minds. With deep gratitude we thank God that the apostasy is not total, the eclipse of the gospel not complete, the abandonment to sin not universal. But the outlook must surely be bleak if our nations do not receive grace to see the vision which once made them the great nations they were by God's grace.

But there is no way out apart from the old vision which God's Word sets before us: God upon the throne; man a sinner in need of gospel mercy; Christ a loving, living Saviour ready to 'save to the uttermost all who come' to him by faith. This vision is what raises men and nations to do exploits worthy of undying remembrance. This is the vision which upheld Luther at Worms as he faced a frowning world. This is the vision which kept Calvin from a quiet scholarly seclusion and nerved him to brave a thousand ills at Geneva. This is the vision which constrained the Oxford martyrs, Latimer and Ridley, to 'light their candle' in Reformation

England. This vision was before the eyes of those brave Founding Fathers who sailed in 1620 to New England. It drove out Carey to India; Livingstone to Africa; Judson to Burma . . . and a host of others to the remotest boundaries of the world.

Without this gospel vision nations perish. When society loses or else rejects the truth of the gospel it slides backward into the vices which disgraced the old world before the Flood and which called down God's fire upon Sodom and Gomorrah. If these societies had known and loved the gospel they would, said Christ, have remained unto that hour (*Matt.* 11:23). The gospel vision is what integrates society, gives it cohesion, unity and purpose. The nation that worships God in truth rides high, conquers its enemies, plants its influence in every corner of the earth, makes its mark in history for ever and for good.

Just so long as any society of men and women is ready to hear God's Word and to shape its life in conformity to it, repenting of sin and trusting in Christ, it is safe. It may be scoffed at as 'primitive', 'old-fashioned' or 'out of date' but it will not lack help from above: 'He shall dwell on high; his place of defence shall be the munitions of rocks: bread shall be given him; his waters shall be sure.' These favours are so because his 'eyes . . . see the King [Christ] in his beauty'; they 'behold the land that is very far off' (*Isa.* 33:16–17).

Never perhaps in our history have we been in greater need of being reminded of the words of Solomon: 'Where no vision is the people perish' (*Prov.* 29:18). It does not take prophetic skill to see that modern society is deeply sick. No simple remedy can put us back on the way to health and recovery. The reshuffling of government ministers cannot do it. Nor the re-drawing of national boundaries. Nor the introduction of new laws – though some new laws (or better still, some of our old laws) are greatly needed. The plain truth is that the vision of God and of Christ has perished from our national leaders almost completely. If we are not vigilant it could slip away even from the institutional churches too.

Modern society is drugged and poisoned with atheism, scepticism, humanism, modernism, postmodernism, nihilism. Men cannot *live* in our modern society but are stifled and smothered. What is called for is a new 'clean air' act. Let in the oxygen of truth and pure religion into men's homes and lives. From the palace to the poor man's attic the nation needs fresh air to breathe and fresh ideas to feed on.

It is time to ring out the old and to ring in the new. To all who have ears to hear we say: ring out the old irreligion, superstition and ungodliness and ring in the gospel of Christ in their place. Let society hear in clear plain language that God is ready to forgive all sin and blasphemy, that heaven and glory are freely offered to all who will repent and come to Christ.

A new millennium looms up before us. It is time to abandon the old visionless paths which have led our civilisation nowhere. The true vision is that which shows us the Lamb upon the throne and all the heavenly host crowning him with many crowns. The ennobling vision is that which points sinners to the cross of Christ and promises peace with God through the blood of Jesus. This vision once flashed powerfully upon the minds of men all over Europe and made it a place of enlightenment to all nations. The vision needs to be seen by us all again, not in Europe only but throughout *all* nations: Jesus Christ is Lord!

Blessed will be the man whom God raises up to preach with great power to a new millennium and to tell men of a

Saviour's grace and love. Meanwhile, blessed are they who persevere in this task in the cloudy day. Sowers and reapers in gospel work are at last to rejoice together (*John* 4:36). After all, only the gospel vision is the truth.

2

Two Steps to Happiness

It is rather surprising that our generation is not a happy one. We have so many advantages that our parents and grandparents never had, and perhaps never dreamed of. Yet we are not happy as a generation. People's faces betray their inward strains and fears. Few smile and almost none sings joyfully.

This is not what we might have expected when it is remembered that only a few years ago politicians were telling us that 'we had never had it so good'. Whatever material blessings we have had in the past few years, they do not appear to have brought much inward delight. The prevailing mood of society is glum. If we ought to learn anything from our experiences of having more worldly goods than our parents did it is surely this: outward things do not make people happy.

It is worth a little time and thought to ask why it is that outward things do not bring satisfaction to the human heart. If man were nothing more than the developed 'animal' that he is reckoned popularly to be, he ought to be perfectly happy in a society where good things are available in plenty. A cow in clover is perfectly content. Why then should mankind not be equally content in a world of eating and drinking, playing and dancing? Why, when man has a paradise of sports, fashions and entertainments on his doorstep, is he still worried and unhappy? Why is he puzzled, angry and afraid if he has ready to his hand everything that his eye and his appetite could ask for? Man is a strange being to be sure.

At the heart of the problem is a mistake in people's basic thinking. It is partly this: Man does not know himself. He does not realise that he is the being he is. He imagines himself to be what in reality he is not. He supposes that he is a material being in the first instance, rather than a spiritual one.

It is easy to see how he falls into this mistake. After all, he is surrounded all his life by material things and so he assumes that he is just material and earthly as the things round about him are. Besides, he is annoyed when he is told by religious people that he is more than merely a body. He scorns the suggestion that he has a soul and is put out when he is informed that he might have to live somewhere after death.

This is the first source of man's deep and almost incurable unhappiness. He does not know himself and so he imagines himself to be what he is not.

The first step towards happiness is taken when we come to know ourselves to be more than a physical body and when we see that we were made for higher things than this world can give us. It is a step towards happiness to recognise that we have a spiritual part to us. As well as matter, we are mind. As well as a body we have a soul. In addition to instincts we have willpower, and conscience and a sense of accountability for how we live.

If we were only 'animals' of a more developed kind, this would not be the case. Material stimulus would then be all that we needed to lead us to complete happiness. But society is discovering by painful experience that to live for bodily appetite does not give the happiness which was expected. When pleasure is over it leaves pain if conscience can tell us that our pleasure was stolen.

To say that we have a conscience is to go far to explaining the widespread unhappiness which we witness today all round us. Conscience is a difficult thing to live with even when we give it its place. This is much more so when men live, or try to live, without reckoning on its importance at all. Conscience in man is a tiger, which growls and mauls him inwardly. It is a fire that burns within him and cannot be extinguished by mere willpower. Conscience cannot be silenced by ignoring it or by wishing it away.

Those who search for happiness and yet live in defiance of their conscience are hoping for the impossible. The art of being happy begins only when we have realised that there can be no happiness until the conscience is at rest.

But how can we get the conscience to be at rest? The first answer which suggests itself to us all is this: we must be good. This is an answer to man's problem which appeals to us all and which sounds obvious. It is mankind's age-old answer to the age-old difficulty which he finds when he takes seriously the fact of his own conscience. It sounds right. 'If I do well I shall have a good conscience and so live happily.' It is not that this solution is wrong so much that it is impossible to us in our present state. For one thing people do not like being good! But even when we are 'good', two difficulties remain which our consciences soon remind us of. What about those times in our life when we were not good? And, can we be certain when we are good that we are good enough? Man might be happy in being good if only he could convince himself that he is sufficiently good. But the more honest we are the more we know that we are not.

To tell people to be good is what bad preachers do every day. One hears them on their radio programmes early in the morning and late at night. One pictures them in their pulpits on a Sunday. It is the downfall of a nation when its preachers tell men to be good.

Of course, there are many more who are telling people to forget goodness and just to get on with the business of being happy. Their message is something like this. 'Goodness is boring. What we all really want is excitement and pleasure.' People can fill in the space marked 'pleasure' with everything they want. It does not matter to those who are promoting the message to 'get happy' how people do this. It can be by drink or by drugs or by all the other hundred and one things advertised to fill the eye and the stomach.

But the problem with all these promoters of pleasures is that they are not, as we said at the start, making society really happy at all. Millions of money are spent every week on going after happiness and yet people are no nearer to getting it than when they started.

The bad preacher and the promoter of pleasure both have this in common, that they are completely failing to make people happy. The bad preacher fails because his message to 'be good' is just too difficult. The fact seems to be that nothing is harder for mankind than to be good. To be good is what nobody really can be and so to tell man to be good is only to mock him and to send him away in despair.

If anyone should ask us why people today look so unhappy, we can only say that it is because they are the victims of a sort of cruel conspiracy on the part of bad preachers on the one hand and greedy sellers of fleshly goods on the other. Between these two, people today are trapped and caught in a vice so tight that they are suffocating. Small wonder if people are unhappy! All they hear these days in the marketplace of life are the cries of merchants peddling their wares: 'Buy pleasures here! Buy pleasures there!' But these pleasures do not all carry a government health warning to say to the buyer that the end of them is bitterness, sorrow and a bad conscience.

Tortured as men are today by fear of what they have done in eating the forbidden fruit of lust and passion, they cower away from the light. Those few brave souls who do in these days venture to hear a preacher usually hear nothing but a dry homily on how to be good. No wonder churches are crumbling and lie empty when the troubled society all around normally finds there no message to heal their wounded spirits or calm their fears!

The first step to happiness is to know ourselves, as we have said. And to know ourselves is to know that we are not good and have very little interest in becoming good. Scarcely one in ten thousand is trying to be good, or is asking how he or she can become good. There must be a second step before true happiness can be found. Something better and more wonderful must be known by man to make him really happy.

The second step to happiness is to seek God till we find him. When we find him we arrive at true happiness forever. Seeking God is not finding him. But it is necessary to seek him if we are ever going to find him. We shall know when we have found God because then we shall be truly at rest. Our heart will be full. Our mind will be persuaded. Our conscience will be at peace within us. Those who find God come to the real secret of all things. They know him; they love him; they enjoy him; they adore him.

When we are first told to seek God we become afraid. That is not altogether surprising because God is not much talked about in modern society. Those who do mention God usually say something foolish or unkind about him. That is a great pity because God is real and he can be known by man in this present life.

That is not pious talk but sober truth. It must be correct. Let us show how. Three arguments may suffice to demonstrate that people can know and love God. First, think of the Christian martyrs. They might have saved their lives by denying what they knew about God. But they preferred to die than to deny what they knew of him. To them it was better to lose their life than to lose God by sinning against him.

Then, look at the stories of wonderful conversions, of which there are many thousands in print. How else are we to explain the way in which blasphemers were changed in one day into devout believers and sinners into saints? It is the power of God which produces this complete change in people's lives.

The third argument is from the rapturous experiences of happiness which Christians sometimes have had and still do have. Some of the diaries of eminent (and not so eminent) believers show that their writers occasionally experience in their lives a sort of heaven on earth. This happiness is not earthly but supernatural. It flows from a knowledge of God and an enjoyment of him in this life.

When we seek God we ask for him first to accept our persons. This is where those preachers go wrong who tell men to be good. They overlook the fact that those to whom they preach have never been good – at least, not good enough. But God will not accept our service or our prayers until we ourselves, as persons, are first acceptable to him. Conscience, if we stop and listen to its voice, tells us all that we are not good enough for a holy God. Poor troubled men and women today need to know how they can have acceptance with God when they are vividly aware of their own evil past.

Seeking God always starts at that very point: 'How can I, who am so bad, be acceptable to God?' Those who never faced this question almost certainly do not know God as yet. The gateway to God and to heaven is right here in this simple question: 'Can God forgive people who are as bad as I have been?' To stand on the threshold of this question is to have taken the first step. At this point a man has seen himself for what he truly is. He has realised that he is not yet fit for God. Happiness may not come consciously when we have taken this first step, but we are on the right path towards finding happiness once we have come to this point. Wonderful as it is to relate, God has done something for man so that man may be accepted and loved by Him. We call it the good news, or gospel. In a word it is this. God has come down to earth in the person of his Son Jesus Christ. Christ gave himself for us on the cross. He died for us to remove our sin. He rose again from the dead to be our living Saviour. He lives today and invites all men to believe in him and find true peace.

To believe in Christ is to know God. It is the second step to which we referred before. Once a man has come to this point his happiness is sure and certain forever.

It is not possible for any person to be inwardly satisfied till he or she knows God. The reason is simple. God made us for himself. Our heart is restless, as a great Christian once said, until it finds its rest in Him. Neither money nor sport nor marriage nor work nor pleasure can *fill* the heart of man. But God can fill it when we come to know him by faith in his Son Jesus Christ.

Have you got this happiness of which we speak? If not, would it not be worth your while taking two steps to get it?

3

Evangelical Compassion

Compassion is one of the loveliest of all the graces, but one which is not often enough talked about. Men pray for love and faith, for pardon and patience. But who prays to be filled with compassion? This virtue is overlooked and undervalued. Yet its price is above rubies. It is an index which measures our likeness to Christ and a thermometer which registers the temperature of our love for souls.

Compassion is that affection of the heart by which we are touched with the plight of others. In a perfect world it would have no opportunity for expression. For where there is no misery there need be no pity; and where men lack for nothing there is no occasion to grieve over their wretchedness. The entrance of sin into man's experience, however, has been many-sided in its effects. It has not only stripped him outwardly of comfort and plenty; but it has also blunted his sensitivity to the point where he feels scarcely any compassion either for his own miseries or the miseries of others. The Christian, whose eyes are open to men's tragic state, cannot look on sinners without deep pity.

Our twentieth century, coming as it does two millennia after the gospel, might have been expected to have brought with it a race of men who excelled all their forefathers in the graces of pity and compassion. But on any review of this century, now drawing to its uncertain close, it has to be admitted that it has proved to be one of the most barbarous and pitiless since time began. Two thousand years of Christian influence have not – alas! – softened men's hearts far and wide, though they have produced, at the same time, wonderful examples of outstanding gospel kindness.

It is worth a moment's pause to reflect on the exceptions which exist to the common rule of moral insensitivity in our day. Here and there upon earth there are devout followers of Jesus Christ, who rise above worldly ambition and self-interest. They do not live for money or pleasure or fame. They do not invest their wealth or their energies in any human rewards, but give themselves night and day to the task (thankless, very often, in this present life) of doing good to their fellowmen, hoping as they do so neither for praise nor gratitude from others.

The angels in their ceaseless circuits around the heavens must marvel at the many acts of compassion which they behold as they look down on our loveless world. What charms these celestial spirits is the patient, unremitting devotion of God's servants as they daily pursue their labours here on earth for Christ.

In a certain city of India (to take one example) live a devout missionary couple, now in their fiftieth year of service. What made them leave home and family to live there among a people not their own and on an income scarcely a tenth of what they might have had in some secular occupation in London or New York? One thing alone stirred and motivated them – evangelical compassion.

Back home in their teenage years in their local church they both, while as yet unmarried, felt the constraining hand of

Christ upon their lives to 'Go and tell all nations'. Now their wizened features and white hair betray the story of their life together as, through thick and thin, they have been faithful to the heavenly vision. A simple brick church well filled with worshippers and a vernacular New Testament, read and stained with tears in many a local home, are the visible, grateful tokens to these honoured saints that their life's labours for Christ's lost sheep were not in vain.

Let us suppose another example. In a small country church, far from the noise and hubbub of the metropolis, there lives and preaches a faithful pastor of God's flock. Many a temptation he has felt to conform to the spirit of the age and to smooth down his message to suit men's tastes. But love of Scripture and the fear of God have kept him faithful to that gospel which is offensive to the natural mind. He has neither profaned God's worship by innovations nor pared away the sharp edges of divine truth. Against all plausible argument he has told himself over the years that it is murder to the souls of his hearers to paint the fair face of truth with entertainment. His best work is done unseen to human eyes: his faithful praying for the people; his patient study of God's Word; his steadfastness in feeding Christ's flock; his pastoral care and patience under provocation. What keeps this man yearly working all hours of the day and night? One thing alone does so – love of his Master and zeal for his people's souls. Men may not see it; but the angels do.

Let us suppose a third example of compassionate love of souls. A Christian woman lives in a poor area of the town. Now long since past her days of youth and beauty she is all alone in her small flat. To her it is more a 'base of operations' than a 'home, sweet home'. The small space which she has around her furniture and her bed are largely taken up with piles of Bibles, books and tracts. These she buys out of her slender income to use on her regular visits to the homes of neighbours round about her. The tracts and other pieces of Christian literature which she has given away over the years in this manner run into some thousands.

It has been the vision of her life to carry the good news of a Saviour's love to the lost. The squalid houses of her neighbours would bear witness, if they could speak, to her Christian charity and winsome evangelistic conversations. She recalls brightly of how richly Christ has compensated her for all her losses as she thinks of the dozen people in her downtown neighbourhood who owe their conversion to her. Such evangelical compassion makes the heavens ring with angels' song.

That there are such persons in the world as those whom we have just described is owing entirely to the example of the Lord Jesus Christ himself. His own sinless soul was filled with the compassion of which we speak. Christ's window on to this life was so utterly different from that through which other men peer. Christ lived as one who had nothing to do all day long but to bless the poor and needy who wanted him. Great men usually spend their time either in waging wars, or ruling empires, or amassing wealth. Jesus Christ spent his time showing pity to men. He devoted his time to the needy. His meat and drink was to raise up the poor, to convert the wicked, to undo the devil's work in men and in the world at large. Compassion was written large over every aspect of our Saviour's ministry.

We must distinguish between that compassion which leads men to perform acts of philanthropy and benevolence and that far higher compassion which constrains Christians to carry the gospel to their fellowmen. Noble as acts of philanthropy are, they do not compare in value with that highest form of philanthropy which stirs God's children to bring gospel light to men. To say this is not to despise what the world calls 'charity'. But it is to say that there is a charity involved in giving the gospel to sinners which exceeds all other forms of charity.

This must be so because only the gospel can cure the evils of man's soul. Only the gospel can reconcile men to God. Only the gospel can bring sinners to heaven and to glory. To give men the gospel is the highest possible expression of kindness. No service we can do could exceed or even equal it. The gospel of salvation brings blessings to those who receive it which are infinitely above all earthly benefits, both in kind and in duration. It is no wonder therefore that gospel philanthropy is the hardest and rarest form of all.

But *evangelical* compassion exceeds all other forms of kindness. Its concerns and constraints go beyond men's present earthly needs, however great, and they have in view the *ultimate* good of sinners – and that eternally.

That such compassion and concern were those of both Christ and his apostles is very clearly seen in the New Testament. Much as Jesus might have grieved to see men's poverty, disease and ignorance, he grieved far more because he 'saw them as sheep not having a shepherd' (*Matt.* 9:36). He saw that they had none to pity their lost condition or to remedy it by bringing to them the gospel message. This is, then, the ultimate human plight of men in this world; to be a sinner without a spiritual pastor, to be speeding towards hell without any to teach or warn, to belong to that mass of mankind which does not know what lies beyond the grave or how to escape it.

Similarly the Apostle Paul was animated by a pity and, a concern for men which sprang from deepest gospel motives. This is evident from the way his spirit was 'stirred' within him when he saw the idolatry of Athens (*Acts* 17:16). The superstition which he witnessed all round him cried out for a remedy which only the gospel of Christ could bring.

This point is still more strongly made by Paul in one extraordinary expression of compassion for his fellow Jews. For them, he informs us, he 'could wish that myself were accursed from Christ for my brethren, my kinsmen according to the flesh' (*Rom.* 9:3).

Perhaps there is no statement in the Bible which more powerfully demonstrates the nature of gospel love than this amazing utterance of Paul. It is, of course, not a prayer but a theoretical wish. Yet it speaks eloquently of the lengths to which love for souls may go. He was, if it were lawful and possible for him to ask such a thing of God, very nearly prepared to forfeit heaven for himself if only he might thereby secure heaven for his fellow countrymen.

It is the mind of a Moses, who could well nigh desire to be 'blotted out of the Book of Life if only the sins of others might thereby be pardoned' (*Exod.* 32:32). It was – still more to the point – the mind of Christ himself, who, in love for sinners, did in very fact bear their sin and drink down the cup of their damnation.

Higher than this it is impossible for love or compassion to go. Only the Lord Jesus Christ could atone for sin. But great souls who are much filled with his Holy Spirit may come somewhere near to his sublime compassion. Moses got close to it. So, too, did Paul. So have many preachers, Reformers and missionaries. So, too, have many Christian women, boys and girls, who have gladly given their lives for Christ in martyrdom.

Unless we are much mistaken, we need, all of us, to get back to this emphasis on evangelistic compassion. It has been the mainspring of all really great service to Christ. The times do not need better methods but better men. Give us Christians like this and nothing will be impossible.

4

A Well Balanced Christianity

The older and more mature we grow as Christians the more we value balance in matters of religion. When we are in the early stages of our Christian life we are apt to be too impressed by what is extreme and by what is excessive. Children, especially when they get together in groups, always tend to raise their voices into a shout. They are at the stage in life when it is boring to talk in a normal tone of voice. So, being easily excited and having the noisy example of one another, they quickly all raise their voices to shouting pitch and sometimes almost to screaming pitch. This extreme of noise adds to children's excitement, and experience suggests that the noise will grow and grow until one or other of them gets hurt and the rest melt guiltily away.

Something like the above happens in churches where immaturity of understanding is the general norm and where there is insufficient good sense on the part of members, and especially of leaders, to know that what begins with excitement today may end in tears tomorrow. Push any doctrine or any practice too far and it will recoil at last and surprise us like the kick of a horse. In our childishness we are apt to think that every good thing is made better by stretching it more and more or else by stressing it more and more. But this is absurd in both natural and spiritual matters. A hungry man is made better by a good meal, but he is not made better still by eating two or three meals at one sitting. A sick man will hopefully recover if he takes his prescribed medicine. But he will hardly recover at twice the speed if he takes his medicine at twice the prescribed rate. Overdoing in medicine, and in religion too, leads to undoing.

To push any point of doctrine just too far is to upset the biblical balance and harmony of the truth. Stress the transcendence (remoteness) of God at the expense of his immanence (nearness) and you become a deist. Stress the immanence at the expense of the transcendence and you become a pantheist. The true doctrine is poised in equilibrium between both immanence and transcendence. This fine balance is to be seen at every point in the biblical presentation of each doctrine. The need for balance must be observed at every point. We are told of a God who is holy and yet also gracious. God is one in essence, yet three in Person. Christ is God, and yet also man. The Scriptures are the Word of God, but they are also the words of inspired men. Christ is the Saviour of the elect, yet he is preached as available for all. We are saved by grace, yet we must observe God's law. As Christians we wait for Christ's return at any time, yet we must study to be industrious and to earn our own living here and now.

The danger is when one aspect of a doctrine is given prominence beyond its biblical balance. Zealous Christians have often laid up a legacy of sorrows for those who came after them because they unintentionally went just too far with a good thing. How else are we to explain the origins of masses and confessionals, monasteries and nunneries, relics and 'saints', pilgrimages and crusades? We find it hard to imagine that these practices came into the Christian church on any other pretence than that they would promote piety and so glorify God.

We do not indeed have to look so far back in history to find the same mischievous tendency at work. Some err by stressing the purity of the church at the expense of its catholicity; some by promoting the church's catholicity at the expense of its purity. There is danger on both sides and a wise leader will be aware of both. There are a score of examples before our eyes of how evil comes from carrying a good thing too far.

Error in Christian doctrine is generally nothing more nor less than truth which is looked at with one blind eye. Error is seldom totally wrong. It is often half-truth which is taught as the whole truth. Take the orthodox doctrine of the holy Trinity, that there are three eternal and equal Persons in the one Godhead. The true doctrine requires that we confess both the oneness of God and also the 'three-ness' of the Persons. To destroy the doctrine of God it is only necessary to close one's eyes to either aspect of the truth. Remove the oneness of God and you have three gods; remove the 'three-ness' of God and you become a Unitarian. The truth lies in the holding in balance of both aspects of the doctrine. Error appears as soon as we become blind to one or other facet of what the Bible teaches.

To say what we have said is to state that error begins in the church as a result of a *false method* of seeking to know the truth. The truth of any doctrine cannot be found by looking at only half of what God's Word tells us about it. Every heretic can find a verse of the Bible to support his heresy. That is not because the Bible is unclear but because each doctrine of Scripture can be formulated accurately only when *everything* that God has said on the subject has been taken into account.

The appeal of every heresy is that it offers a quick and easy way to the truth. It short-circuits the process by which true religion is to be known and understood. The ignorant and the unwary are snared by the zealous cult leader because he can 'prove' his errors by quoting two or three texts of Scripture. However, he does this stealthily and craftily because he conceals from his hearers six or seven other texts of Scripture which define or qualify those which he advances as 'proof' for his error.

The hallmark of any true doctrine is that it satisfies the evidence of Scripture entirely and in every place. The doctrine of the holy Trinity is just such a doctrine. It explains every text of Scripture that bears on the being of God.

The same is true of the magnificent doctrine of the Person of Christ. What hammering on the anvil there had to be in the Early Church before this piece of sublime theology was understood and defined to perfection! Thousands of texts and parts of texts had to be weighed and pondered, discussed and debated before the church finally formulated the biblical doctrine of one Person of Christ in two natures – and all that is implied in so high a mystery. The true doctrine of Christ's Person is the greatest wonder of the world. Our familiarity with it ought never to blind us to its exquisite harmony and balance. Disturb the doctrine at any point and the biblical Christ is lost – and, oh, the loss!

We have argued that truth is to be sought only by keeping in mind all that God has said on any particular point and that biblical doctrines are always in a state of balance. We have further affirmed that truth is lost and error introduced as soon as we become blind to any aspect of the truth. The great systems of error which men have erected over the centuries have all gained the support which they have had (and may still have) because they affirm one aspect of truth at the expense of others. This is certainly true of Arianism, which reduces Christ to something less than God; and of Arminianism, which robs God of his free and sovereign will to determine all future events. It is, furthermore, true of Romanism, which builds the church on one who is not Christ; and of Ecumenism, which promotes church unity by denying the church her creed. In all these erroneous forms of Christianity the harmonies of truth are upset. Men have distorted the fair face of Scripture and dislodged the balance.

What theologians have done in the realm of theology, Christians may do in their own personal relationship with the truth which they hold and profess. Let us suppose that, by God's rich grace, we have come into a sound church whose creed is orthodox. We believe in the doctrines of grace and subscribe to the Westminster Confession, or to some similar body of Christian doctrine. A new question now faces us. Do we relate sincerely and honestly with what we profess? The thought cannot be a new one, but it may require some explanation.

A harmonious Christianity takes more forms than that of sound theology. It involves a right attitude on our part to the theology which we profess. If the creed which we believe is false then our religion will be in vain. But if our relationship to our orthodox creed is wrong, our religion may be equally vain. The harmony which is in mind here is that between what we officially profess and what we inwardly believe. There must be a real correspondence between outward confession of doctrine and inward conviction of that doctrine. Experience teaches that this is not always so for various reasons.

Some subscribe to what they do not really believe because they have not thoroughly understood it. Some subscribe to creeds which they dislike in order to get a stipend. Some subscribe to a creed because they grew up with it and only realise later in life that it was not truly their own *personal* creed. Some subscribe to a good creed, without ever having been convinced that it reflects the teaching of the Word of God. This last sort spend their latter years attempting to amend their creed, usually from within the ministry of a church which subscribes to it.

There is, however, still another way in which there needs to be a balance or harmony in the Christian life. It is the balance between our inward beliefs and our outward circumstances. This, one suspects, is the most difficult and elusive balance of all because it involves our emotions of fear and hope. The subject is difficult but it is important and rewarding.

Our faith in the true God and our knowledge of his will ought to give us peace in all the situations of life in which we ever find ourselves. Our creed is so full of reassurance that, if our faith could only reach to the right level, we could never be much troubled by outward circumstances. Though the heavens should fall we should be at peace. Though the mountains were cast into the sea we would be inwardly calm and unperturbed. This is so because what we believe is more than sufficient to counterbalance all the outward miseries of this world. If God be for us, if all things work together for good for us, if Christ died for us and intercedes for us, if God never leaves nor forsakes us, then what outward thing in all the world can have the power to do us any harm? This is the logic of faith and it is sound sense.

The painful awareness we have, however, that we are not always inwardly at peace is the proof that there is disharmony between what we *say* we believe and what we really *do* believe. When our circumstances steal away our inward peace, it is a sign that we lack faith in God. 'Where is your faith?', asked Christ of the disciples in the storm. They had faith but it was in a dormant state when outward circumstances appeared menacing.

Our own experience of fear and discouragement as Christians pulls us up sharply with the realisation that our own souls are not so much influenced by what we profess to believe as we may think they are. We are not all at the place where we can affirm with Paul: 'I have learned in whatsoever state I am, therewith to be content' (*Phil.* 4:11). In his storm (*Acts* 27) he was in perfect peace; but, in our storms we are not. In the Apostle Paul there was a wonderful harmony of doctrine and practice. There was remarkable correspondence between what he believed and the state of his soul in the midst of threatening circumstances.

Surely this is the very point at which we are to work as we work for more sanctification. Our aim and our prayer is that we might more perfectly reflect our creeds when we come face to face with our crises. In the storms Little Faith has much misery because he sees little of God and is soon terrified. Great Faith sees God in all events and believes that sunshine will soon follow the rain. Both have faith, but the latter lives in a more constant peace because outward trials are better balanced by inward trust in God's promises.

Tremblingly we pray, 'Let me henceforth do likewise.'

5

God's Thoughts – Far Different from Man's

G od at first made man in his image; and man since the Fall has been re-making God in his own image. From this flow most of the evils and miseries of man's life. It is the fountain from which springs all idolatry and it is the fuel that feeds all unbelief and contempt of true religion. If mankind could ever be persuaded to think of God aright, evil would virtually cease. But this cannot happen till the end. Meanwhile one generation after another continues to have low views of God, supposing that he either does not see them when they sin, or does not care. It will be not the least shock experienced by evil men at their death that God will say to them, 'Thou thoughtest that I was altogether such an one as thyself' (*Psa.* 50:21).

At our conversion we begin to see God in a true light. Dimly at first, but yet truly, we perceive that he is different from all other beings. Before we have grace we treat God as little more than a polite name. But after we enter his kingdom we realise that he is real, powerful, holy and worthy of our deep trust. Yet even now we have only a hazy understanding of God's dealings with us. Like children, we look at everything from our own standpoint. We learn to talk of God's lordship and sovereignty, but we use words whose meaning largely escapes us. Our thoughts are as yet little shaped by the Bible. The very young Christian is as yet incapable of thinking of God as the one 'of whom, and through whom and to whom are all things' (*Rom.* 11:36).

Growth in Christian grace is closely related to our growth in theological knowledge. If our progress in doctrine is poor, either because we hear poor preaching or do not care to read books on Christian doctrine, we shall hardly advance in a true knowledge of God and of his thoughts. Doctrine, after all, is just a word for God and for his works and ways as these are divinely revealed to us in holy Scripture. And ignorance of God is, of all forms of ignorance, the most serious and the most common. Conversion brings to us a true and saving knowledge of God, but it does not remove all our ignorance at a stroke. Conversion is the first knowledge of God. It is real light, but it is as yet only the peep of day. Vast increase of light and knowledge are possible to the converted man. Such increase is to be achieved as a rule only by deep and prayerful study of the Bible and the great books such as Calvin's *Institutes* or the writings of the Puritans.

When we are well and truly launched on our way as life-long readers of the Bible and of the best books, we are struck by the difference between God's mind and ours. It is as though his thoughts are the very reverse of ours. If God's thoughts are wise, we discover, then ours are folly. The Bible's way of talking and reasoning is at almost every point the opposite of what we might imagine or expect.

A cursory look through the Bible may help us to see how different God's thoughts are from ours. Why should God choose to create the universe in the six working days of a week? The history of human thought and philosophy shows that this procedure on God's part has been felt to be very disagreeable and offensive. That God should create in many millions of years is far more acceptable to human wisdom. And why should God create the woman from the rib of the man? Does not that insult the dignity and spoil the equality of the woman? So the wisdom of this world argues. And why should God destroy all the human race by a flood and spare only the eight persons in the ark? Few narratives in the Bible have met with more indignation and scorn than that of Noah and the flood.

Hardly have we recovered from the surprise of the flood when reading through the Old Testament than new shocks are in store for us. The Tower of Babel. How hard it is for man's wisdom to accept this as the origin of the human languages and the formation of the ethnic groupings which we call 'nations'!

But worse shocks await us. God's wisdom passes by all the nations of mankind before Christ and gives the blessings of salvation and heaven to just *one* family, that of Abraham. No saving mercy is shown to the mighty world empires of Egypt or Babylon, Persia or Greece. For two thousand years, no less, the grace of God runs in the one tiny channel named Israel. What Socrates, Plato, Aristotle and the great geniuses of the pagan world saw and understood was, and is, in many respects useful knowledge. But their combined wisdom was foolishness in all the great matters of salvation and eternal life. The light which they had was, in terms of its religious value, sheer darkness. It did not begin with the true God and it did not lead men to him. The only light there was in those Old Testament times was in David, Isaiah, Amos and the other prophets. No philosopher can tell us why God chose the Jews. If clever men had planned the history of our world, it would have been very different!

Let us come down to the life of our blessed Lord Jesus Christ. Once again, the paths chosen by God's wisdom are 'past finding out' and his ways are inscrutable. The Messiah, predicted from the foundation of the world, comes into history in a manner which offends all our human wisdom. He is born in a stable. His mother knows not a man as yet. Even Joseph is, for a time, confused and perplexed. No trumpets sound loud from the balcony of heaven to tell the universe that the long-awaited Saviour is born in Bethlehem. A few pious and poor shepherds receive a bright angelic visitation. Some wise men from the East follow a star. But the rest of the world is oblivious to the coming of the Lord of Lords and King immortal. Bethlehem sleeps as soundly as ever that night, not knowing that 'the hopes and fears of all the years are met in [her] tonight', as Phillips Brooks so poignantly expressed it. How different are God's thoughts from men's!

The life of the Lord Jesus is a catalogue of surprises from start to finish. Human wisdom has shown what it would like to do to 'improve' on the real Jesus. The apocryphal (spurious) Gospels invent a boy-Jesus who forms clay pigeons and makes them fly! The fruitful imagination could invent very much more to the same effect. But the real Jesus did no miracle till he received the second degree of unction of the Spirit at his baptism at the age of thirty. How those thirty silent years tease the inquisitive wisdom of scholars! If only they could find out what Jesus the child or Jesus the teenager was like! But the wise God kept his beloved and holy Son as a 'polished shaft' in the quiver of almost complete secrecy till the age of thirty (*Isa.* 49:2). The one glimpse we do have of Jesus is at the age of twelve and it shows us that he knew then his own identity and his mission. O sublime wisdom of God!

It is disconcerting to human wisdom too to notice how very close to death and difficulty Christ lived all his earthly life. Scarcely is he born than Herod's agents come to kill him (*Matt.* 2:8). His first sermon at Nazareth is so unpopular that his fellow townsmen would have killed him on that very day if supernatural power had not delivered him (*Luke* 4:30). Almost from the start of his public ministry he is marked out by the religious experts of the day for venomous opposition (*Mark* 2:6–7). He is opposed, argued with, doubted, tempted, provoked, misunderstood, vilified, conspired against.

The three years of his ministry are one long blaze of divine glory and goodness. But such was the wisdom of his critics that they would have him denounced as a very instrument of Beelzebub and special agent of the devil (*Matt.* 12:24). The surprise is not that after three years and a half he was put to death. The surprise is that they let him live so long, bearing in mind the intensity of their hatred of him and the immense power which was at their disposal (or so they thought) both to end his life by decree of their General Assembly (*John* 11:53) and to destroy faith in his resurrection from the dead by falsifying the evidence which supported it (*Matt.* 28:13).

The Apostle Paul tell us, when we proceed to consider the death of Christ and his cross, that it is *the* contradiction of all human wisdom (*1 Cor.* 1:19). Indeed, the cross as a way of pardon is as far removed from man's idea of a gospel as the north pole is from the south. It is 'foolishness' and 'a stumbling block' (*1 Cor.* 1:23). The cross is wisdom of such an unfathomable kind that it beggars the human mind. 'How can this man give us his flesh to eat?' (*John* 6:52). How, asks the mind of man, can a dying Jesus who cannot save himself be an almighty Saviour who can save us? None of earth's princes understood this mystery when they led away Christ to be crucified (*1 Cor.* 1:25). If this Jesus were sent from God, they argued, God would not have left him to die in torment and in darkness.

The Apostle Paul gives us the key which turns in the lock and opens for us the door of *real* wisdom: 'For after that in the wisdom of God the world by wisdom knew not God, it pleased God through the foolishness of preaching to save them that believe' (*1 Cor.* 1:21). The cross is foolishness. But, being *'God's* foolishness' (*1 Cor.* 1:25) – what a phrase! – it is wiser than all the wisdom of all the cleverest scholars who ever lived, or will yet live. God, in his wisdom, has saved the world from sin by that method which seems to the human mind most absurd and improbable: God punishes his own Son *for us!*

When Isaiah, in the Spirit, informs us concerning God's thoughts that they are not our thoughts (*Isa.* 55:8) he tells us what is true everywhere in the Bible. Every doctrine is included here: creation, providence, election, reprobation, substitutionary atonement, heaven and hell. At every point God's wisdom is vastly brighter and better than ours.

To have come to see that God's thoughts are far different from ours is to have taken a quantum leap forward in understanding the doctrines of the Christian faith. Those who get to this point – and, sadly, not all do – look at their Bibles with new eyes and with new adoration. They see that of themselves they know nothing aright and are but babes and fools in their own understanding. They realise that the only solid wisdom which men possess is what they get from a study of the Bible and from nowhere else. All other wisdom, be it never so highly rated by men of this world, is nothing but folly.

To come to the point at which we are content to believe and live by the wisdom of God's Word alone is so spiritual a step that we must not be surprised to find it in only a choice few in this world – and not in them perfectly. To reject human wisdom is about the hardest thing that fallen man can do. We call it repentance and it is a duty which remains to be done all our life and every day of life. To believe what God's wisdom reveals as the substance of our creed and as the rule of our duty is what we call faith. It is intensely difficult to fallen man.

The best theologian is the one who most perfectly traces out the mind of God in Scripture; and the best saint is the one who most closely obeys the rule of duty laid down in Scripture. To do either is impossible till we have learned first to crucify our own wisdom, to live unconcerned about the opinions of men and to look for that honour that 'comes from God only' (*John* 5:44).

To draw a little closer to these mighty and blessed objectives is a thing devoutly to be aimed at every day we live.

6

Why Spirituality Comes First

It is hard to say what Christian spirituality is. It is not equivalent to giftedness because there are eloquent and talented people who are full of themselves. It is not the same as theological exactness because those who are less correct in their understanding of the truth are sometimes strong in grace and love to Christ.

Spirituality is not something which can be measured by studying one aspect of a person's life but by taking account of all aspects. It is roughly equivalent to what we mean by 'Christian character'. It is the measure of our spiritual renewal after the image of Christ himself.

Our assessment of our own and others' progress in spirituality must begin with the realisation that there is a basic distinction to be made between what a man has by nature and what he has by grace. One man has a naturally clear intellect, another a naturally accurate memory, a third has a naturally charming temperament. These are all valuable assets but their possession does not prove spirituality, still less spirituality of a high order. It proves natural charm and natural talent and nothing more. Such talent is to be found also in the unconverted.

Spirituality, however, is proved by the presence in the soul of those graces which are not natural. These are such characteristics as humility, fear of offending God, delight in communion with Christ, love of souls, ambition to glorify God and to enjoy him, love towards other believers as one's brethren, repentance for all known sin, frequent confession to God and longing for the eternal state of glory. Such things as these cannot arise out of natural inclination or temperament because they require the supernatural energies of the Holy Spirit to produce and promote them.

There is, of course, an infinite distance between what is natural and what is supernatural. The two do not shade off the one into the other. The least Christian is in a different category from the most devout non-Christian. The work of God in the most charming and respectable unbeliever is not qualitatively as excellent as the work of God in the weakest of his own true children. The lowest spark of grace in any man places him in a spiritual class far above all natural excellence. 'That which is born of the flesh is flesh; and that which is born of the Spirit is spirit' (*John* 3:6).

It seems to human wisdom to be offensive to say that a man cannot cultivate himself so as to be pleasing to God. After all, man *can* pray and preach, read the Bible and take the Lord's Supper, go to church services and even become an authority on some aspects of religious study. But all of this falls short of spirituality because it is not the outcome of that act of the Holy Spirit which we call the new birth and which alters a man radically in his whole nature.

To be religious and not spiritual is to be in the most dangerous state of soul possible to man in this life. Christ has the sternest warnings for such persons. He denounces their religious condition to be that of whited sepulchres (*Matt.* 23:27), persecutors (*Luke* 11:47–51), hinderers of men from salvation (*Luke* 11:52), hypocrites (*Matt.* 23:13f), 'serpents' and a 'generation of vipers', who cannot 'escape the damnation of hell' (*Matt.* 23:33).

Such language is a reminder to us that a purely nominal religion is worse than useless. It is a fearful snare to the soul and leads away from God under the pretext of serving him. It causes 'the light in us to be darkness' (*Matt.* 6:23). It leaves us children of the devil while we imagine ourselves the children of God (*John* 8:41,44). It will at last shut the door of heaven forever against us even though we have convinced ourselves that we are safe (*Matt.* 7:21; 25:10–12).

Let a man become a church member without the new birth and the probability is he will be secure in his church membership till he wakes up in a lost world. Let a man become a preacher, a divinity professor, a missionary, a church historian, a moderator, an assembly clerk, a printer of Bibles – all without the new birth – and such persons are only twofold more the heirs of hell than they would otherwise have been (*Matt.* 23:15). However hard it is for us to take in this doctrine, there cannot be the least doubt that it is the plain and obvious teaching of Christ in many places of the Gospels.

Spirituality therefore comes first and must be put at the top of all our priorities. The preaching of our blessed Saviour is remarkable for the emphasis it places always on the need for man to be spiritual. The beatitudes, for instance, are a word picture of the spiritual man. Then, too, the judgements Christ passes on men's behaviour and men's attitudes show that his all-seeing eye searches after one thing in man – spirituality. When a person came to him with spirituality of soul he received commendation and blessing. When any came without it they departed much as they had come.

A lack of spirituality is the hidden cause of so many of the evils which vex the church of Christ. It accounts for a great deal of the theological and spiritual confusion to be seen on every hand. It explains how leading churchmen can deny the virgin birth and scoff at the physical resurrection of Christ. It accounts for the way in which churches subscribe to orthodox articles of faith and then ignore them in practice. It is the reason why office bearers take vows at the time of ordination and then conveniently forget them. It explains how those who are high in church office can on occasion be low in personal integrity. It accounts for the way men may hold the mystery of the faith with an uneasy conscience and with a bad reputation. It accounts for all the compromise and all the moral fudging we see in church and state. Unspirituality is a taproot of every sort of hypocrisy and duplicity. There is little hope that society will 'get back to basics' till it is faced up to and dealt with biblically.

There are degrees of spirituality among those who are spiritual. The new birth makes all those who are the subjects of it into spiritual men. But spiritual men differ in their measure of spirituality. The difference in this case is that of the measure of their progress.

It is all too possible for us to judge incorrectly as Christians. Our habit is too often to judge by men's natural talents rather than by evidence of their inward grace. It is surely to warn against this tendency that our Lord informs us that 'the last shall be first, and the first last' (*Matt.* 20:16). Our Saviour's meaning must be that Christians whom we place high in the scale of eternal rewards will often be among the lowest, and *vice versa*. This text is full of deep interest and should constantly remind us that the world's judgement of spiritual things is worthless. Even as Christians we often make an assessment of men which is very defective. In the judgement of Christ many a humble widow and many a praying mother will enter into the kingdom of glory much ahead of some who in this life have been biblical scholars perhaps, or popular preachers.

If spirituality is first in importance, it follows that it should be that which we seek first for our own souls. It involves the active and deliberate co-operation of the Christian with those processes of grace within him by which he becomes ever increasingly renewed into the likeness of Jesus Christ. In particular, it may be viewed as a bending of every part of the soul towards the one aim of living unto God in this life.

Spirituality comes to us with difficulty and it involves us in costly self-discipline. It is a discipline, however, which yields precious fruit and well repays the effort. Each faculty of the soul needs to be daily schooled to behave in a particular way. The intellect (or mind) has to be daily trained to absorb the truths of holy Scripture till the habit of our thoughts is to judge all we hear and see by Scripture light. We cannot trust the judgement of the press or the media too far. The Christian must constantly unscramble the maze of facts which he hears, and attempt to pass all that he knows through his mind in the light of holy Scripture.

The feelings and emotions also of a self-disciplined Christian must be trained to react appropriately. Our emotions ought to vary as we hear and read God's Word. The promises of God are to evoke comfort, gladness and hope; the threatenings of Scripture should lead us to tremble and respect the justice of God; the laws of God should make us strict and dutiful, and they ought to fashion our conscience till it habitually loves obedience and protests at lawlessness. The will-power of the Christian requires to be daily urged to perform each duty till it is done as well as strength and time will allow. Of course, when all is done we shall still need to remind ourselves that we have done nothing yet as we ought to do and that we are, at best, but 'unprofitable servants' (*Luke* 17:10).

No small part of spirituality consists in our attitude to ourselves. Here is where the difference between Christian and Christian betrays itself. It is painful but essential in our progress towards true spirituality that we should mortify our natural excess of self-love. This begins with the way we think of ourselves and ends with the way we speak of ourselves. The pattern we must follow is that of the Apostle Paul who admits to a constant warfare in his soul against his own corruptions (*Rom.* 7:14f) and whose self-judgement is that he is 'less than the least of all saints' (*Eph.* 3:8), 'the chief of sinners' (*1 Tim.* 1:15) and 'the least of the apostles' (*1 Cor.* 15:9). Such language is genuine evangelical humility. It is not the false modesty of religious formality but the realisation, which we should all heartily share, that apart from God's grace we are nothing.

The day has come upon the church of Jesus Christ in which it is imperative that we should all strive after much spirituality. We are facing extraordinary moral and spiritual opposition on many sides. Only a spiritual approach to the evils around us will be sufficient to carry us safely through. Weak spirituality is crumbling before our very eyes in so many churches. The walls are sinking because men built them of sand. Christ did not suffer and die to beget a perishable church but an imperishable. O let us cry to God to give us a sufficiency to stand and to withstand in this evil day! If spirituality is our main study how can we fail?

7

The Romance of Christian Faith

One sometimes meets Christians who use scriptural words and thoughts with no more feeling than if they were licking stamps. They seem to belong to a religious world whose citizens live always north of the Arctic circle of emotion. Their spiritual affections are buried beneath yards of ice and snow. When they venture to talk about the things of God they use good words and express sound ideas, but they are evidently in complete control of their own emotions always. In such company the doctrines of God's Word have the fascination of an ice crystal or a snowflake. The truths of Scripture look beautiful but feel icy cold. One senses that it would be an impertinence to breathe a sigh in their presence or to utter a stifled sob. To shed a tear would be unpardonable.

No doubt emotion can be overdone in religion as in all else. Not everything we say on biblical subjects need be said in a gush of tears or punctuated with a solemn Amen. We concede readily that some spoil our appetite for holy emotions by their working too hard at them. We remember hearing of a preacher whose every sentence almost was greeted by an Amen from someone in the gallery. It was perhaps tolerable, if only just. But the voice in the gallery gave itself away at one point in the service by shouting Amen when the number of the next hymn was announced. The ardour was artificial. It was scarcely more significant as an expression of religious feeling than a twitch of the face or a nervous habit of coughing. For false emotions of this or any other kind we make no appeal here. But we do put in a plea for more expressions of genuine emotion both in the pulpit and out of it.

Dare one venture to state that it is scriptural and sound for a Christian to give vent at times to profound religious feelings? Admittedly, allowance must be made for temperament and for the differences between national characters. The 'stiff upper lip' is part of some nations' philosophy of life. Other countries have no such tradition. No one doubts that maudlin sentimentality is a weakness. We are right to dislike and distrust it. But great natures are capable of great feeling and no subjects under the sun should rouse us to great feeling like the subjects of which our Christian faith speaks: the being and attributes of God, the eternal decree, the covenant of grace, the person and work of Christ, the judgement to come and the life everlasting. To think and speak of these transcendental themes in a matter-of-fact way is to betray a fearful meanness of spirit and smallness of soul. All subjects of divinity oblige us to awe and reverence by the very majesty of their content.

It is not difficult to show from Scripture that outward expressions of emotion are proper and right at times. Saintly men whose calling in life involved them in great responsibility and self-control are occasionally represented in the Bible as overcome with profound feelings, either of sorrow or of joy.

No one who has read the story of Joseph's self-disclosure to his brothers could ever forget the power which this passage possesses: 'Then Joseph could not refrain himself before all them that stood by him . . . And he wept aloud, and the Egyptians and the house of Pharaoh heard . . . And he fell upon his brother Benjamin's neck, and wept . . . Moreover he kissed all his brethren, and wept upon them' (*Gen.* 45:1, 2, 14, 15).

Nothing in this lavish outpouring of emotions has any connection with emotionalism. It is a scene of holy and spontaneous affection, the springs of which are both earthly and heavenly: love of his own family so long parted from him; delight at seeing Benjamin, pleasure at hearing that his father is still alive; inability to do other than forgive their past conduct towards him; realisation that his brothers were better men than they once were and, above all else, a sublime realisation that God had fulfilled his earlier dreams by giving him pre-eminence over his brothers. Never do our feelings rise so high as when we come to some such great crisis or climax in life. When God's hand of providence becomes visible we must have a sense of destiny which stirs us to the depths. If we are not so stirred we must be either little men or men of stone.

David's emotional experience must be safe for us to learn from, not least because he was a 'man after God's own heart'. The various inflections in David's feelings are worthy of more study than they have received. His affections were as capable of variation as the melodies which he played on his well-tuned harp. To our information in the Books of Samuel must be added all that we learn out of the Book of Psalms. The emotional life of this holy man was played out on an instrument of ten strings, now soaring to the heights and now plunging to the depths. We may select one incident out of many to illustrate this emotional side of the Psalmist: 'O my son Absalom, my son, my son Absalom! would God I had died for thee, O Absalom, my son, my son!' (*2 Sam.* 18:33).

Again, as with Joseph above, we must see here spontaneous and profound feeling. David is more violent than Joseph. This is partly, perhaps, because he was a man of war, but partly too because the occasion of his emotions was much darker. He saw the sin of Absalom, his beloved son, as the immediate cause of death. But David perceived the finger of God to be pointing also at his own prior sin with Bathsheba. It was one of those moments in life which possess a high sense both of drama and destiny. The 'sword would never depart from David's house' (*2 Sam.* 12:10). God was pursuing his quarrel with David and the recent dramatic death of Absalom was a poignant reminder to the king that every syllable of God's Word is as right and just as it is inescapable. The tears which flowed down the face of that noblest of men were salted by thoughts of self-reproach more than by anything else. It is those who love God greatly who smite most violently on their own breast when they see what their past folly has brought on other men's heads.

The Apostle Paul is the greatest example we possess, apart of course from Christ, of a man in whom strength of intellect and strength of feeling are matched. He is the living proof, if proof is needed, that logic and emotion are not mutually inconsistent. No man ever lived who was more perfectly the clear-headed theologian and the calm biblical scholar while at the same time the passionate lover of Christ and souls. Where truth and souls were at stake Paul was immovably firm. On Elymas the sorcerer he can pronounce a fearful woe as we read in Acts 13:10–11.

It is the same holy indignation which constrains him to warn the Galatians twice over: 'Though we, or an angel from heaven, preach any other gospel unto you than that ye have received, let him be accursed' (*Gal.* 1: 8–9). This is emotion, a sanctified jealousy for sound doctrine, mingled with indignation at the audacity of the false teachers who were ready to invent 'another gospel' (*Gal.* 1:6). The church of Christ could do with a baptism of this holy jealousy for God's truth at this present hour.

Let it not be thought for one moment that Paul was a 'hard man'. With young converts he was as tender as a nursemaid with her children (*1 Thess.* 2:7). Even as he warned them away from error he wept, shedding tears of sorrow for those who are spiritually blind: 'I tell you, even weeping, that they are the enemies of the cross of Christ.' (*Phil.* 3:18). He speaks of 'serving the Lord with many tears' (*Acts* 20:19), of 'warning every one night and day with tears' (*Acts* 20:31) and of writing to believers 'with many tears' (*2 Cor.* 2:4).

Paul sighed as he prayed for the conversion of the Jews (*Rom.* 9:1–2) and 'travailed in birth' till 'Christ was formed' in his converts (*Gal.* 4:19). His own great heart beat in fullest sympathy for the saints, whatsoever their feelings were (*2 Cor.* 11:28–29). He yearned for the spiritual good of every particular believer 'in the bowels of Christ' (*Phil.* 1:8). 'The love of Christ constrained' him in all his labours. The world was his parish. Holy desires for God's glory and man's good poured out of his soul with immense energy. It is hard to say whether passion for truth or passion for the lost is the stronger emotion in his life. No doubt they were both mighty in him.

In the examples we have taken of holy men in whom emotion and feeling were strong, we have confined ourselves to men of like passions with ourselves. It would not, however, be difficult to show in the life of our blessed Lord himself that emotion and feeling were an integral part of his experience on earth – albeit in his case the emotions were sinless. Our Redeemer knew emotion in its complete spectrum from darkest gloom and sorrow to ecstatic joy and rejoicing. His sympathetic compassion draw tears from him at a graveside (*John* 11) and over poor, blinded Jerusalem (*Luke* 19:41). Our human miseries were his daily concern whilst here below. Nothing that touched mankind was an irrelevance to him. If his more frequent emotions were of sorrow because of man's piteous plight, he was no stranger to times of joy also (*Luke* 10:21). All this he voluntarily undertook for us, for his eye was on the prize of all these sufferings – the purchase of a church to be his bride. This was the 'joy set before him' for which he 'endured the cross and despised the shame' (*Heb.* 12:2).

To our mind the evidence is compelling. Emotion is a proper part of the Christian's life. It is not to be stifled but educated. We are not to teach ourselves how to suppress our feelings but how to express them unto edification, both our own and others'. To that end we would offer the following suggestions.

1. The Christian would do well to make it his habit never, if possible, to speak or think of God without deep reverence and affection. At least, he should refer to God feelingly when his circumstances permit him to do so. Let him set before his mind the greatness of his debt to God both for his birth and for his new birth, for his election from Adam's fallen mass and his redemption by Christ. He should set aside time regularly to meditate on the truths most fitted to excite and enthral his soul. What moves one man may not move another. Let each Christian dwell frequently on those texts, doctrines and experiences which much excite and enliven his own heart and set in motion the wheels of elevated feeling.

2. Then, we would suggest that the Christian should avoid all excess of laughter, or at least, such laughter as is associated with trivial amusement and worldly humour. There is laughter which flows from pure spiritual joy. It is probable that we cannot have too much of that. But it is not common. The habit of laughing at the slightest opportunity is not only unedifying to others, but also it is harmful to the cultivation of the profounder emotions of the soul: awe, fear of God, sense of the nearness of Christ's Spirit, gravity and nobility of character. It ill befits the princes of a great King to laugh over trifles. They are likely, if they do so, to appear to others to have forgotten their station in life and their high standing.

3. We believe that it is good for the soul to develop the habit of expecting to feel great emotion from time to time in the use of the means of grace, especially under preaching, in secret prayer and at the Lord's Table. The habit we refer to is to expect that God will periodically fill our hearts with wonderful melting and heavenly comfort. We believe that those who do not expect such experiences are not likely to have them. But this is much to their loss. Christ is able to fill the heart to overflowing by his felt presence and grace. The great saints of the past have had frequent experience of such gracious visitations and we are to seek to grow up into Christ as they did till we have similar spiritual exercises.

4. In conclusion, we should not seek God for the sake of gracious experiences but rather seek God for his own sake. A child who loves his mother does not love her company for ulterior motives but for love's sake alone. So the Christian delights in God for no other reason than that he is God, most delightful to contemplate and most worthy of our highest affection and obedience.

There cannot be any serious doubt that the romance has gone out of the Christian life for too many believers. We have forgotten for too long that every doctrine of Scripture should have its corresponding echo in the soul. Truths of theology are not bare philosophical speculations but powerful influences. 'The words that I speak unto you, they are spirit and they are life' (*John* 6:63). A large part of the Christian's joy and comfort is to 'feel' the force of these truths and to become familiar with them till they fill his heart with their heavenly music.

When doctrines are preached with feeling, warmth and passion they will be felt in the pew, not by all, but by those who have a soul which thirsts after God. Those who blow the gospel trumpet have the highest privilege on earth. It would be good to see congregations everywhere thrilled and excited by the Word of God. Such emotion is sanctifying and exhilarating. It is also infectious.

Christ counted it his joy to save us from sin. We should count it our joy to suffer on earth for his sake. Once we come to that point we have recovered the romance and may well be close to recovering the blessing also.

8

First Learned – Worst Learned?

The Jesuits, though a most deplorable society, have given us one of the most important insights we possess: 'Give me a child till he is seven years of age, and then do what you like with him.' They have had the acuteness of mind to see that what we learn first we learn most formatively. Our mind and body, soul and heart, conscience and religion are all moulded for good or ill at the dawn of life, while every part of us is soft and plastic, easily shaped by adult hands and fashioned by our whole environment.

It is not our intention here to speak only on the upbringing of children, but it would be wrong to leave the application unmade. Christian parents ought to look upon the first seven, or ten, years of their children's life as crucial in their development. It is in these years, if ever, that the child needs to be surrounded by all that is wholesome, healthful and helpful to body, mind and soul. These are the years which make or mar the character. Too much love and protection there cannot be in this period of the child's life. Due firmness and due discipline there must be also. Good habits must now be taught to the child. These should include respect for elders, attention to the Bible at home and in church, regard for the Lord's Day, regularity in prayer, grace before food, a pattern of sleeping and rising, and a realisation that the world we live in is for work rather than play.

The sad but well-known fact is that many parents today are too selfish or too busy to put in the time and effort needed to mould their children's characters into proper shape. The average modern child, like Topsy, might well say, 'I 'spect I grow'd'. 'Growth' there has been, but of a sort that owes less to parental care than to casual influences: programmes on a screen, playmates down the street, comics picked up at random, ball games day and night, scraps of popular cunning in a society seeking survival. Nothing about righteousness; less than nothing about God; absolutely nothing about Jesus Christ. Whilst the average church-going family is much above this standard, there are too many Christian homes where children get only minimal care and instruction.

If, as we have said, it is true that what we learn first we learn best, it must also be true that what we learn first, when wrongly taught, we learn worst. Bad habits learned early are hardest to correct in others and in ourselves for the simple reason that they have been with us longest and so are most deeply ingrained in our nature. This fact, it seems to us, is one reason why there are so few great and saintly Christians met with in our age. Converts today are often called by grace from worldly, ill-trained backgrounds in which the first patterns of life and thought have been formed under non-Christian influences. As a consequence, when they come to Christ (say, at the age of twenty) they have a whole twenty years of paganism, practical and theoretical, to unlearn. In the weak climate of modern church life, they will probably meet so few outstanding Christians that they will not rise above mediocrity. Thus mediocrity becomes the norm and unconsciously perpetuates itself.

The lesson from this to Christian parents is surely obvious. If this vicious circle of mediocrity is to be broken, our young children need to be brought up in a way rarely met with today. Our Puritanism needs to come down from the book-shelf and become a living force within the home once again. We do not have in mind the revolting thought that parents are to groom their sons to become a generation of 'Little Lord Fauntleroys'. But without forcing the rosebud unnaturally, it is possible for believing families to set high Christian standards before children's minds at an early age.

Nowadays the church of Christ needs a fresh crop of excellent men like William Perkins, Matthew Henry, and Robert M'Cheyne to raise the standards. Whilst only God can give children saving grace, we as parents can see to it that they have all that common grace can give. This must mean that what they learn first they learn well. When by grace they are later converted, they have then already got a mind well-stored with Scripture and sound doctrine and a lifestyle which is in clear outward accord with the law of God. From such homes do great saints come.

The danger we have drawn attention to has a very considerable bearing, too, on the duty of the local church as well as on the Christian home. All too often the standards are set in a local church on the tacit assumption that the voice of the people is the voice of God. Nowhere is this seen more clearly than in matters of church worship.

If our cherished theology is to bear fruit in the lives of the rising generation, it must find fuller expression in our church worship. Sad to say, it happens all too often that the fine theology of the Reformers is reflected in the sermon, but not in the substance of the prayer nor in the materials of our singing. This must produce a hybrid type of Christian worship, in which the sermon looks to Calvin and to Geneva, while the singing looks to Campus Crusade and the endless singing of choruses.

What we sing to God can be almost as influential in the development of Christian character as hearing sermons. The proof of this is to be found in any prayer meeting on earth. People quote from their manuals of praise as often as they do from the Word of God itself. They may even use expressions drawn from Scripture and phrases taken out of their chorus book in the same prayer, even when these are inconsistent with one another. The fault surely lies in the practice of the local church in their not ensuring that in the service of God's house nothing but the best is allowed to be used.

What converts first learn from their churches they will very quickly learn to regard as the norm. The Jesuit principle will apply every time. While converts are still young and therefore new to the faith (whatever their church back-ground), they will be ready enough to learn to correct their previously bad habits of worship. They are still young enough in the faith to be open to biblical influences in the church where they are converted. But this teachability will harden in a few years' time. What they find at first they will, in most cases, come to regard as normal and right, without examining theological principles of worship for themselves. For this very reason it is a church's wisdom to keep everything out of public worship which has no good warrant to be there. It is a thousand pities if what our converts first learn in God's house has to be some day regretted.

It belongs to the genius of biblical religion and of the Reformed faith to aim at perfection, since that is the character of the God whom we serve. It is not enough to have men and women brought to a profession of trust in Christ. Our aim is to 'present every man perfect in Christ Jesus' (*Col.* 1:28). This is a mighty and a strenuous task, but it is the task of the Christian and of the minister. Conversion is to be viewed not as the end, but as the beginning. Our converts have to be shown the best example as well as fed with the best teaching that we are capable of giving them. This must surely have been the goal at which the Apostle Paul aimed when he advised his converts to 'mark them which walk so as ye have us for an example' (*Phil.* 3:17).

The bearing of this upon our subject must be clear enough. If our churches are to grow in grace and spirituality, they need more than sermons and sound worship. Even when these great mercies are to be had in a congregation, they are not all that is required for the health of the church. To excellence of preaching and of worshipping there needs to be added the excellence of exemplary living. Surely this is the reason why Paul's epistles contain so many references to ethical duty.

The first and second chapters of Titus may serve to illustrate this point perfectly. Titus' commission is, among other things, to 'set in order the things that are wanting' (1:5). All was not done when elders were ordained, nor even when the mouths of unruly deceivers were stopped (1:5, 10–11). The purity of the church and its preservation in health cannot be maintained by the appointment of office bearers alone, or by the orthodoxy of its teaching ministry. More is needed. Hence Paul proceeds to lay down ethical guidelines for the membership of the church, especially for persons of more mature age. The 'aged men' are to be exemplary (2:2) and the 'aged women likewise' are to act in a manner which 'becometh holiness' (2:3). They are to 'teach the young women' (2:4) by precept and by example how to adorn the doctrine of the gospel. 'Young men' are to be similarly 'exhorted to sober-mindedness' (2:6). Not only by preaching is this to be done. Titus himself must 'in all things show himself a pattern of good works' (2:7). The lesson is clear: example is infectious.

Our modern churches make a good deal less of the place of holy example than they should. The effects are often all too visible. Gravity and sober-mindedness are scarce virtues. Elderly Christians of exemplary spiritual character are all too few. It is small wonder if young converts, having nothing higher to look up to than one another, have been allowed to take their standards from themselves. Again, what has been first learned has generally been worst learned. A better way has not occurred to anyone in the fellowship, and so standards are allowed to slip to something just above the level of the world outside.

The challenge of our day is for some who love the truth to consecrate themselves to God with exceptional dedication. They would need to deny themselves and take up Christ's cross in an uncommon measure. They would need to be early and late at the Word of God. They would require to learn the meaning of that mortifying expression 'fasting and prayer'. They would have to live above the crowd and be oblivious to its sneer. They would need to be men of vision and of perseverance as they tread the steep upward path. They would have to aim for a more mature godliness than they have witnessed around them. But they would have at last their reward. They would shine like stars in all our modern churches. They would raise the standards and show how much holiness is possible to sinners on earth. Brainerd is gone, and M'Cheyne is gone. Who is yet to come?

9

What Is a Christian?

To define a thing is not to understand it or to explain it. Human words are little more than labels which we use to stick on our thoughts. They are like coins minted by the human mind and passed into common circulation to facilitate the commerce of speech and friendship. But, just as few who carry coins understand the complex world of banking or finance, so few who use human words think much about their meaning. We speak of the sun, but who can understand the marvellous processes by which it rises and sets, bringing light and cheer to every creature? We speak of marriage and love, but behind such simple words is a mysterious web of emotions that we can explain scarcely at all. How do two hearts become intertwined? How can two persons become 'one flesh' and be committed to each other for a lifetime? What unseen instinct leads a woman to 'leave her father and her mother', whom she has known for twenty and more years, and follow a man whom she has only known for five years, or one, or less? Who then can tell us what it is to be a Christian?

Nowhere is our vocabulary so insufficient as in the things of God and of Christ. Doubtless those who are counted worthy to go to heaven will marvel to discover when they arrive in glory that God is immensely different from their thoughts of him here in this life, and far, far better. Not one of all the billions of sinners, saved and unsaved, who have used the word 'God' over the centuries has ever used the term with a true understanding of what He is like.

The same might be said of everything to do with God. We speak of the Trinity, but what true conception do we have of the ineffable mystery of a God who is three in one? Neither Athanasius nor Augustine nor Calvin knew the thousandth part of what they meant when they confessed and affirmed 'the holy Trinity'. They admitted this themselves in what they wrote. They did not pretend to explain what they wrote about, but did not wish to be 'wholly silent' on these lofty subjects, as one put it. So what then is a Christian?

Our best thoughts of God come as far short of their glorious reality as a child's understanding of higher mathematics, astronomy or brain surgery. The point comes home to every parent who enters the primary school and looks at the pupils' work on the classroom wall. The drawings of men and houses, hills and rivers are recognisable as primitive attempts to portray reality. But how crude they are by comparison with the masterpieces of a Leonardo or a Rembrandt! And how crude are the efforts of these masters themselves compared with the realities which our great Creator has made! Just as our ideas of God are only crude and ill-shaped attempts by sin-retarded minds to conceive of him as he really is, so is our notion of being a Christian.

To state matters in this way is not to suggest for a moment that a Christian's thought of God is all wrong and therefore worthless. Every Christian mind has a true knowledge of God, just as every primary school child has a true knowledge of his or her own mother's face. But our perception, though true so far as it goes, is only a pale shade of the reality. The point of saying this is not to deny that we know God but to remind ourselves that God is immeasurably better than our knowledge of him and to whet our appetite to know him better than we do in this present life.

The Bible itself makes much the same illustration as we have used when it informs us that at the moment 'we know in part' and we only 'see through a glass darkly' (*1 Cor.* 13:9, 12). The point being made is that earthly knowledge of spiritual reality is very imperfect. The knowledge of God which we possess is valid but by no means complete. Our present level of understanding in the things of God is good and sufficient for us while we are still in our childhood state on earth. For here we understand and think 'as a child' (*1 Cor.* 13:11). But in the world to come we shall have knowledge of God and of the purposes of God which vastly outstrips what we can expect to attain to at present. In the future state we shall think 'as a man' (*1 Cor.* 13:11). There each one of us shall be a perfect Christian.

The means of grace, so necessary to us in this life, are a glass in which we behold the glory of the Lord and are changed 'into the same image, from glory to glory' (*2 Cor.* 3:18). But we shall need no such glass in the world to come. There we shall see 'face to face'. Knowledge of the Lord then is to be immediate and direct. Here, meanwhile, it is mediated to us through a variety of God-given influences and agencies: through the created order, through mind and conscience, through law and authority, through prayer and meditation, above all through the sacred Scriptures and their faithful exposition by God-sent preachers.

It is because they were aware of this difference between earthly knowledge and heavenly knowledge that some of the old Scottish Covenanters, when mounting the scaffold to die a martyr's death, bade farewell to the Bible as well as to their families and friends. Their intention was to remind themselves and their hearers that the Bible's light will not be needed on the other side of death. There they would 'know even as also they were known' (*1 Cor.* 13:12). Faith's light is that of the candle; heaven's is the radiant splendour of the meridian sun. To pass from grace to glory is to take a quantum leap, not only of comfort and of delight, but of knowledge and of understanding. As the enormous telescopes of our famous observatories magnify by many hundred diameters the sizes of the planets above us, so our comprehension of the ever-blessed God and Saviour shall suddenly undergo at death a dramatic enlargement. There and then we shall know Christ, not as now from afar and in the Book, but as at hand and by direct sight.

This full and open sight of Christ in glory, which the saints are to have, will certainly bring with it a whole new world of love and emotion to their hearts. Not that it will be absolutely and entirely new, because they have the first stirrings of it already. But as love grows by knowledge of the one loved, so our love to Christ will undergo a powerful magnification and intensification when he lies open to our wondering gaze. With rapt attention and breathless with adoration the whole church in glory will see at last into the meaning of all its theology in a moment and forever.

One element to be fully seen by the saints must be the entire sovereignty and fullness of their own salvation. If this is seen by some of them already in this life, it is certainly not seen by all of them, nor is it yet adequately seen by any of them. But the sight of a Christ covenantally given by God to be the Redeemer and Husband of some sinners and not of them all will be more proof of absolute divine sovereignty than all the writings of the theologians of this world.

Then every saint will feel the full force and exquisite meaning of Christ's own words: 'Ye have not chosen me but I have chosen you' (*John* 15:16). This will excite within every bursting breast the yearning to exclaim: 'Unto him that loved us, and washed us from our sins in his own blood, and hath made us kings and priests unto God and his Father; to him be glory and dominion for ever and ever. Amen' (*Rev.* 1:5–6). Why such a God should love one and not another sinner, when neither was better than the other, cannot be unrelated to the ecstatic gratitude of this doxology. The saints find themselves in heaven, they know not how or why except by God's free will which is his love to them. Eternity itself will not make this mysterious choice by God any less marvellous or adorable in their eyes.

Then, too, the vision of a Jesus on his Father's throne will clear up all the errors of Christ-denying sinners at a single stroke. The eternal Sonship of the Lord Jesus; his absolute equality with his Father; the merit of his passion and blood-shedding; the completeness of his victory over sin, Satan and the grave; the security of the Church which is the ransomed prize of his agony and self-offering on the cross – all these and all related truths will be cleared up in the twinkling of an eye for every believer. His eyes shall drink in the panoramic spectacle of a Saviour in the midst of the throne of God. Then no Peter will thoughtlessly reproach the Lord with his, 'That be far from thee, Lord.' No Thomas will doubt. No mother of a John or a James will utter their over-ambitious prayers. No praises will be shared with saints or angels. No 'Hail Mary' will jar the seraphic anthem. God in Christ will be all the theme of all their praise.

Sin will then be seen in all its sinfulness as the contradiction of God's will and the provoking of his holiness. For only when Christ is fully known can God be fully loved for his burning purity. And only when God is so known can the sinfulness of sin be understood. Sin will be remembered in heaven. But it will be no grief to saints because it will be seen in the light of a redemption completed by a visible Christ. And as the sight of Christ will evoke our utmost assurance and affection, so the love of the Spirit will be endlessly poured upon our hearts and our Heavenly Father will ever speak words of peace and welcome to us. We shall know evil in that day only from the standpoint of good.

Furthermore, we shall at last and in the presence of Christ understand 'the manifold wisdom of God' revealed in the church (*Eph.* 3:10). The church has been the most mis-understood institution on earth. Persecuted, rejected, afflicted, misrepresented in all ages, the Church of Jesus Christ will at last, and in his nearer presence, be vindicated and justified. The destiny of the people of God is to be one of final triumph. The laughter of saints will be inevitable when they see in that day how true and faithful God's words have always been. In their marvellous perseverance and eventual home-coming the angelic host will see God's many-sided wisdom displayed and exhibited in all its labyrinthine intricacy.

Each saint's conversion is different; each saint's experiences different; each saint's labours different; each saint's gifts different; each saint's enjoyment of Christ different; each saint's death and judgement different. Yet all the saints together will be happy, holy, heavenly, harmonious.

It is a church worthy now of such a Saviour and of such a God. Who then can say what it means to be a Christian?

THE STRUGGLE OF FAITH

10

The Vulnerability of True Religion

Hardly anything in this world is more liable to damage than true religion. We find it in the Bible, we read of its having made its appearance at favoured periods of history and we discover it still in choice places. But it is a rare and exotic plant whose delicate petals are early bruised and whose fragrance is quickly destroyed by man. This observation is much the same as that of a noted Highland preacher of old. Asked if he had any complaint against Jesus Christ, he replied: 'Yes, that he comes so seldom and stays so short a time'. It is the wealth of men and nations when Christ comes to dwell among them. But it is all too easy to drive him away. He will not stay long where he is not loved and wanted, and when once we have grieved him to depart he takes away with him gospel, church and grace.

When we here speak of true religion we mean something more and better than what is commonly understood by the term 'Christianity'. We refer to Christianity in its best and highest form, in which its professors glow with ardour for the Word of God and are fervent in their attachment to one another; where accuracy in doctrine is matched by mutual love and mutual trust; and where the aim of all is to excel in spirituality and obedience. Such is the Christianity that Christ brought to earth. It is seen in the apostolic churches in large measure, though even there it is marred in many ways either by error in the head or by error in the heart or by both.

Not that true religion began with the New Testament. Its first original was in paradise where our first parents, as yet strangers to the Fall, walked with God and worshipped him with unsinning consecration. At that time true religion was natural and came easy to man. Though the period of its existence was brief, it was heavenly. The heart of man revolved round its Maker and instinctively sought and found its full happiness in him. At that period of man's history – the only golden age our world has yet known – all religion was pure and perfect. No idol had yet been made or even conceived in the imagination. The bright image of the invisible God shone perfectly in Adam's soul, and was reflected in his every thought of God. Every kindness of God's providence at that time was matched in man by an answering gratitude. Man's first religion was the perfect mirror image of the glorious being of the Lord their God.

After the Fall man's religion had to change to suit his altered circumstances. Blood must now, and for many centuries to come, be shed on many altars to teach the worshipper that he approached a Deity whose majesty he had offended and whose justice required to be placated. Our fallen parents must now be clothed with skins as a sign of their need of Another's righteousness, now that their own was wholly lost. Their religion now must be built upon the promise of a coming Deliverer who should one day crush the Serpent's head and do so after intense suffering on his own part (*Gen.* 3:15; *Rom.* 16:20). True religion after the Fall all hangs on the hook of sovereign grace and it must be bathed at every point in the fountain of Messiah's blood. It is henceforth not obvious or natural to man but comes to him as mystery that he cannot understand apart from an act of heavenly enlightenment.

It is this fact which explains more than anything else can do, why true religion has always since the Fall been so vulnerable. God's truth and worship since the Fall are things that man in his present state cannot begin to understand.

Fallen man sees the gospel all upside down. He makes no sense of it and so he must reinterpret it and rewrite it. It is this fact that explains why all through history, from Cain's day to this, men have perverted God's religion and – left to their own light – they always will. The history of religion is the history of abominations.

At certain points in the past these abominations were visible and tangible. God was represented under grotesque statues and worshipped by grotesque rituals. The Old Testament reference to these is fully supported by what we know of religions, past and present, in countries outside the knowledge of Israel. Nothing so perfectly betrays the inner depravity of man's heart as the record of his religious ceremonies. These are either ugly or cruel or lewd – and frequently all three at once.

At other points in man's history, especially in lands favoured with the Word of God, these external inventions of man's debased imagination are suppressed, only to resurface in other forms. In the case of Sadducaism it was by a denial of the supernatural. They believed neither angel nor resurrection (*Acts* 23:8). They were the Rationalists of their day. In Pharisaism this tendency to distort true religion took a rather different course. The adherents of their movement converted the religion of God's Word from a method of grace into a system of human merit. They gloried in the *form* of the true religion, but they knew nothing of its inward *power*.

The result in both cases was much the same. Souls were robbed of a knowledge of God and religion was robbed of its chief excellence, which is its ability to convert the soul. True believers who lived in the days when Pharisaism and Sadducaism were prominent had to live outside the sphere of religious officialdom and they had to find food for their souls elsewhere.

The above remarks have their applications of course to many situations in *Christian* times also. Again and again God's true worshippers have had to go 'outside the camp' (*Heb.* 13:13) of official religion to find fellowship and so as to enjoy real worship and to meet true godliness. The pure religion of one generation becomes the false religion of another. And sometimes this change comes about in one single generation. The battle cry of a Luther, or Calvin, or Knox, may quickly become merely the *slogan* of a later age. The words are the same but the fire has gone out of them. What came from a renewed heart in one age came only from a carnal heart at the later stage.

The church of Christ has always, and rightly, striven to preserve its religion pure and entire in after times. For this reason it has compiled its creeds, confessions and catechisms. These documents have, in God's mercy, done much to help Christians to transmit pure religion to posterity. But even the best of creeds have not been able to guarantee the permanence of truth. The fault is not in the creeds but in the heart of man. The best of men may have perverse children, and the best ages of the church are sometimes quickly followed by men who undo all that their forefathers did and unsay what they said.

The explanation for all this is not far to seek. No element in true religion is palatable to the natural man and some of its elements are specially distasteful. Consequently the truths of Christianity, embraced and loved as they must be in all the best ages of the church, can only be thought cumbersome and unwelcome to professing Christians living in, and anxious to be conformed to, a more decadent age.

The beliefs and practices of the fathers, however excellent, are often in such days referred to with scorn as mere 'traditions'. The robes of their fathers' religion, too big for the pigmy generation that follows, are cut down to a miniature size. To strive to reach their stature would be too much like hard work for a Christianity that half-loves the worldly mammon. Only one course is open for such men to follow. They must sneer at everything that belongs to the past and shrink their fathers' religion down to their own capacity.

To say all this is not to pretend that there is nothing in the religion of the fathers that could not be improved. Our argument is not that in every possible way 'the old is better' (*Luke* 5:39) but that we should not discard anything from the religion of our fathers without good reason. Too often the old is thrown off because it is too good and because it makes demands upon men's lives which a later age is not prepared to tolerate. We suspect that this is the real reason why the religion of the Reformers and Puritans has frequently since had a bad press. Theirs was a religion so close to the Word of God and so very nearly that of Christ and the apostles, that it has chafed the shoulders of all Laodicean Christians ever after.

It is a pity that more research has not been done on the theme of religious declension. Granted that it is not so important as the theme of revival, it *is* important and has lessons to teach, which we dare not ignore. The ways by which churches and individuals lose their grasp of the gospel must be an instructive one. We offer some brief suggestions as to how this process takes place.

The highest expression known to man of the Christian religion – so it seems to us – is what we refer to as Puritanism. It is that religion which embraces the whole counsel of God, strives to obey all God's known will for man, to have God glorified on earth and which believes in his familiar dealings with the soul here and now. Wherever this religion is found it tends to give to men a heaven upon earth of assurance and godliness.

But as soon as a later generation emerges which resents the theology of the best days, men speak unkindly of it and take steps to modify it to suit themselves. The first casualties are always much the same. God's sovereignty in election and reprobation is eroded. The uniqueness of Christ's person and work is downplayed. The place of the Moral Law in the believer's life gives way to undefined 'love'. Grace is valued less than education. Sermons are listened to rather out of duty than profit. The church ceases to be the centre of men's lives, and scrupulous obedience to scriptural commands is bartered for a convenient accommodation to the standards of the world.

These outward signs of declension are the visible fruits of a deeper problem within the soul. This is a mysterious subject and one not easily understood by man. But it appears that the silent change of attitude from a more to a less spiritual generation happens in some such way as the following.

The best generations of Christians are filled with grace and with the Spirit of God. As time goes on, however, this level of excellence suffers decay and loss. The rising generation differs from the preceding one as silver from gold, and that which follows differs again as brass from silver. The same truths are believed and taught, but not with the same power or passion. God is not so clearly apprehended within the heart. Truth is not so precious. Prayer and fellowship with Christ are not such high priorities. The forms of religion are as yet unchanged but their power is greatly diminished.

The next stage is easy to predict. Where people have ceased to be excited by their creed they will sooner or later revise it downwards. They often do so under pretence of 'improving' it, or of 'returning to the early church', or of 'removing old traditions', or the like. Sin in the heart works deceitfully. It will not at first reject the Word of God openly in case it loses the respect of others. But as time proceeds the process of amending and revising the true religion gains momentum. From being ashamed to touch the creeds and confessions of their fathers men at last grow confident. In the end they throw off all pretence and openly disavow those very doctrines which once formed the very constitutions of their own churches. There is scarcely a church or denomination under the sun which does not bear witness to this process of decline. It begins, as all declension begins, when men cease to *love* the truth.

This downward tendency in the human heart accounts for all the religious errors of the church, and of the whole world indeed. The plain fact is that truth and pure religion are such high, holy and heavenly things that man *cannot* love them till he is brought under the power of divine grace. Even then, man is so liable to decline in grace that he can hardly bear true religion for very long. Two generations, or perhaps three, may hold fast to a sound creed. But for more than three generations to retain the truth without serious loss is remarkable and it is rare.

The above sad fact explains the shrewd saying that 'every institution sooner or later becomes its opposite'. If we confine the application of this saying only to churches, we see at once how just it is. Every church, more or less, that we know of in history has ended up by disowning its original creed! It began by admiring the Scriptures and it ended by rejecting them. It began admiring Luther, or Calvin, or Wesley, or some other great leader of the past, and it ended up by turning its back on all that they taught! The church began with one creed and before long it had evolved another, which was virtually the contradiction of the first. No doubt there are here and there exceptions to this rule. But they cannot be many.

The only way to keep churches and groups of Christians sound is to keep their hearts lively with grace. Nothing else will preserve true religion. Neither creeds, nor university divinity departments, nor historical knowledge, nor extensive learning, nor anything else will keep right religion in the midst of a company of professing Christians if they have once lost their love of the truth. The rule is simple and it is never-failing: If men do not love a doctrine they will not long keep up their attachment to it. The earth will cease to go round the sun before that rule is rendered obsolete.

If true religion then is so vulnerable, it is clear where our first duty as Christians lies. It is to watch carefully and daily over our affections. The moment we suspect that our love of Christ is waning we must cry out for grace. If our love for any point of truth becomes dim, we are to cast ourselves to the ground before God, fearing lest he should give us over to our hardness of heart. All this is deep and humbling work. But it is the only way to hold true religion fast. The alternative is to 'lose our first love' (*Rev.* 2:4). Not for nothing does the Spirit of God say: 'Keep thy heart with all diligence; for out of it are the issues of life' (*Prov.* 4:23).

11

The Danger of Becoming Battle Weary

There are not wanting here and there the signs that good Christians are suffering from a kind of spiritual metal fatigue. In our fellowships iron rarely sharpens iron any longer. Much preaching that is orthodox lacks that ring of conviction which is needed to thrust it home into sinners' consciences. A guilty tameness smothers our zeal. Prayers are humdrum and predictable. The apostolic fire has died down and looks like dying away. The gospel, even where it is preached at all, is clothed with the impeding garments of excessive politeness and respectability. Our sermons are frequently no more than a gentle homily or a quiet talk about good religious ideas. Slowly and imperceptibly evangelical people are coming to terms, emotionally and intellectually, with the spirit of the age. Though we should not care to say so, we nonetheless betray our inner despair of ever seeing revival, or even a reversal of the present trend downwards.

This weariness of soul is not difficult to explain. A deep-seated disappointment has paralysed many Christian people in our day. Both preachers and hearers are disheartened. The recovery of the doctrines of purer orthodoxy some thirty years ago has not yet been matched by a recovery of spiritual power or influence in society. The world passes by the doors of many excellent churches with as much unconcern today as it did when the old theological liberalism reigned in them, and before new and biblical ministries began in them. Preachers who deserve to be listened to by a thousand have to be content with less than fifty hearers.

The vision which many had only a few years ago has not been realised. The mirage has not yet become a pool of water. The promises of God are seemingly at variance with his providences. A bewilderment and a confusion has come upon us. There is a widespread feeling that something has gone wrong. Meanwhile we all grow older. There is an unspoken agreement that the fight is too hard for us. When shall we be able to withdraw from the scene of battle with at least some semblance of honour?

Spiritual drowsiness is very catching. The air soon becomes heavy with it. Active life and movement, once so noticeable, gradually dies down as one after another succumbs to the spirit of drowsiness. As the voices of young children in a nursery die down one by one at their rest time, so the once active testimonies of God's people become gradually silent in a sleepy time.

The Bible portrays for us times when the people of God enter into a period of collective sleepiness. The age in which Moses was born was such a time. Israel had settled down in Egypt. Even their hard servitude did not take from them a love of the Egyptian lifestyle. They were very loath to follow Moses out into the wilderness. They had dreamed too many this-worldly dreams to want to give up the leeks, the onions and the garlic for the uncertain prospect of receiving their promised land. Four hundred years in Egypt had sent Israel fast asleep.

The days of the Judges were another period in which the church of God was largely asleep. It is amazing to us as we read the Old Testament to see how flagrantly Israel was disobeying God's Word at the period of the Judges. They appear to have been blind to the plainest teachings given so recently by God through Moses. Even some of the Judges themselves had serious blemishes in their faith and conduct. 'Every man did that which was right in his own eyes.' If we require an explanation for the state of life at that time, we must surely put it down to a widespread and almost universal soul sleep.

One might have hoped better of the church in New Testament times. But it was not to be so. For a thousand years, till Luther woke up with a start in Germany, the European church slept soundly while Bible, gospel and grace lay hidden out of popular sight. Only here and there was there a warning cry from some remote Italian valley or passing Lollard preacher. Europe, however, as a whole slept on. Dark night covered the one continent of mankind which ought to have carried the torch of gospel truth to every corner of the globe.

It is solemn, too, to recall the words of Christ which inform us, evidently, that the very last period of world history will again be characterised by widespread spiritual sleepiness: 'They all slumbered and slept' (*Matt.* 25:5). Not only the nominal church, represented by the five foolish virgins, will be asleep when the Bridegroom returns; but also the true church herself, though certainly prepared, will have sunk down with weariness and drowsiness just before the wedding day dawns.

The above instances – not the only ones we could cite – are evidence enough to remind us that a blanket of sleep may fall across large parts of the visible church in some ages. This is a sheer fact of history and one which the Word of God presents to us for our warning. No doubt there are many who sleep in the best ages of the gospel and under the liveliest of preaching. No doubt society is at best little more than half awake at any time to the moral and spiritual duties of God's Word. Nevertheless, it would seem to be a clear lesson of Scripture that some ages are marked by a sleep that is well nigh universal.

Sleep is a remarkable phenomenon. It is a kind of animated death. In sleep we are oblivious to the real world. The thief may be at the door, or the fire already running up the curtains of the bedroom. But when asleep we neither notice, nor know, nor care. On the other hand, in the dreams of sleep we care for what is unreal and delusive. Men flee from savage beasts, or fall from cliffs, or sail to treasure islands. Our attention is taken up with what is fictional and fictitious.

Just so is the sleep which comes upon men's souls in ages when the gospel is weak. Armies of heresies threaten the church and people of God; but the church's watchmen are so fast in slumber that they neither realise nor care. When here and there a faithful voice is raised in warning, there is a general outcry and a demand for the maintenance of silence. Or there may happen some scandalous abuse which threatens to mar the church's reputation and her credibility. But when sleep has laid the faculties of the soul to rest, men resent the unpopular question and seek to smother the healthy spirit of enquiry. Nothing is so unwelcome to a sleepy man as the alarm which summons him from his bed.

When soul-sleepiness is widespread, men are all taken up with childish dreams and empty trifles. They make great sound and bluster about small matters of procedure and right order. But they may as easily overlook the great matters of justice, mercy and truth as those Pharisees who 'strained at a gnat and swallowed a camel' (*Matt.* 23:24). The cry of all – or almost all – is for more sleep, and woe be to him who tries to wake them!

None who is even half awake needs to wonder what the explanation is for the state of our modern societies. True religion is banished from the schoolroom and from the media. The slaughter of aborted infants proceeds like a daily holocaust, Governments meet to legislate away the Sabbath and to decriminalise sodomy. Leprosy is breaking out in every limb of the body politic and there is no physician to heal us. Scarcely a voice is raised in high places to call us to repentance. Such voices as there are, are either not heard or else not heeded. Poor nations! Alas, that so great a civilisation as ours should be so deep in spiritual slumber!

It is not surprising that evangelical Christians at this hour should feel numb with battle fatigue. It is no great miracle if they too, catching the general spirit of drowsiness, are tempted to give in to unresisted slumber at this hour. But this is what we must at all costs refuse to do.

By some means or other Christians must contrive to stay awake and on their feet in these days. If, in order to do so, we must cast out the television set or cut off our right arm, we had better do so. To fall asleep at this hour is treason to Christ and to our own souls. It is to lose our 'full reward' (*2 John* 8) or, worse still, to lose our reward and our soul altogether.

The way to avoid sleeping when poisonous gas fills the room is to run for fresh air and to breathe deeply. We owe it to God and to our salvation to run for fresh oxygen for the soul in this present crisis. What is to stop us all from a radical re-appraisal of our present lifestyle?

Instead of meeting for merely social purposes, might we not as Christians meet to read good books to one another? The time which we have formerly devoted to easy viewing and listening, might we not devote, in part at least, to secret prayer or family prayer or neighbourhood prayer? The hours which have been spent cruelly criticising the preacher could in future be put to better use in the careful study of the Westminster Confession and Catechisms. Some of the energy formerly spent in excessive recreation and socialising might be more productively spent visiting the widows in their affliction (*James* 1:27) and in comforting the downcast.

Above all others, preachers must cry to heaven for grace to stay awake at this hour. Let them plunge their heads in the cold waters of God's truth till their dreams of worldly ease are thrown aside. Never did the world more urgently need an awakening ministry than now. Never was there a more crucial hour for lifting high and blowing loud on the gospel trumpet. All heaven watches as we strive to keep awake while all others sleep. It will stand to our eternal credit if we keep at our post. Sooner than we think perhaps may come the dawning of a new and better day. The wakeful servant must one day sit in honour at his Master's table (*Luke* 12:37).

12

Dealing with Our Deadness

When one calls to mind the greatness of our privilege as Christians and the abundance of God's grace, it is marvellous how dead we normally are. While with our heads we subscribe to a large list of doctrines, we appear to pass most of our time under the power and influence of none of them. The problem appears to be that we are, in some manner hard to explain, unable to rise to an exhilaration of mind and soul appropriate to our privileges. Only now and then, so it would seem, do we meet with a Christian who works out his salvation in a way which strikes us as consistent in point of ardour and spiritual fervency: a Paul, an Augustine, a Luther, a Knox, a Whitefield, a M'Cheyne, a Billy Bray. We feel a guilty consciousness in the presence of such men (at least, so far as their lives come down to us in writing) because we are aware in them, and in men and women like them, that their hearts burned continually with holy fire. Ours, on the other hand, do so only feebly and intermittently.

But is it right that we should feel guilty for not experiencing more warmth of heart and affection towards God than we generally do? Is it not too much to ask of ourselves that we should be ever ardent in our feelings and in our attitude towards heavenly things? We do not think so, and that for several reasons. First, we are to remember that the 'first and greatest commandment' includes the obligation to love God 'with all the heart and with all the soul' (*Deut.* 6:5). This duty cannot possibly be carried out without our having lively and active feelings towards God. Indeed, if we were to begin to keep this commandment as we should, then we would need to reach the point at which we direct the energies of our soul towards our Creator with a constant flow and, as it were, in an unfailing stream. The fact that we do not do so ought to be a burden to us which drives us to pray that more divine fire and life may be poured upon the altar of our heart.

A second reason why we cannot excuse ourselves for our habitual spiritual dullness is that Jesus Christ, who is our model man, had none of it. Our blessed Saviour was a burning and a flaming torch of zeal towards God. He was always alive to God his Father, always zealous of God's law and jealous of God's honour. He was ever vibrant in his preaching and witness, ever searching in his judgement of men and their motives, ever fervent for the gospel and ever compassionate towards the lost. Anything like deadness of soul is absent from Christ. The Gospels carry no record of it because they mean us to believe that it was uniquely absent from his perfect character. The kingdom of God was everything to Christ. For its sake he came into the world, fulfilled all righteousness, wrought miracles of every sort, entered at last into death and the grave and then triumphantly ascended to the right hand of God.

To be a follower of Christ must mean that we not only take the blessings of his kingdom gratefully but that we also walk in the footsteps of his zeal for God. This we shall do very largely in the measure in which we are ourselves filled with the Spirit of life and heavenliness. We need to be controlled by the same love for God, even if in lesser degree, which he had and still has. The fact that our own souls are immeasurably less full of heavenly zeal and life than his was while on earth must be a matter of constant sorrow to us. Here, alas, the true explanation for our unfruitfulness is to be found. It is painful to face up to but most necessary, if we are to make any improvement.

A third reason why we must feel consciously guilty of our spiritual dullness and stagnation is that it is a contradiction of all that we profess to believe. Every word of God is instinct with 'spirit' and 'life' (*John* 6:63). All the doctrines of Scripture therefore tend to excite holy affections and to kindle fire on the heart. It is folly and brutishness in *us* when truth comes cold to us or when we go away cold from it. The unwelcome fact, in all such cases, is that we have not 'listened' to the truths which we have heard and that we do not fully believe what we believe.

Oh if only we might receive fresh power to appreciate all that we already know! Oh that we might know what we know in a way that we clearly do not yet know! Oh that the meaning of what we profess would dawn upon our spirits with sevenfold greater force and influence! The real reason, one fears, why so many Christians today clamour for new revelations and new prophecies is that their hearts – and perhaps ours too – have never been gripped by the grand old truths of the Bible. Those who like Bunyan and Spurgeon have found the doctrines of grace to be a treasure-house of interest and delight will never wander off into the by-paths of human speculation or pretended prophesyings.

It is a healthy exercise to examine ourselves as to the spiritual vigour of our souls. No true Christian, of course, is wholly dead to God. But the degree of our liveliness differs greatly from Christian to Christian. It also differs in the same Christian from time to time. We offer the following two tests which we might profitably use for this purpose of examining the measure in which our spiritual life is in exercise.

1. What is it that excites our minds?

The believer knows by experience that he often reads his Bible and prays out of a sense of duty, but then attends to worldly things with relish and even excitement. If we were more alive to God it is certain that this would not be so. What excites the mind most must surely be what we most love. Why do we not find as great excitement in heavenly things as in earthly ones, except that our souls are slow to the one and find the other congenial and therefore preferable? Few who love sport have to drive themselves to the practice field or to the match. But many who love Christ have to drive themselves to their knees and to their closets. Earthly pleasures come easy and spiritual ones come hard. But a wise man will take steps to chide himself for this and he will bend his soul towards correcting this disgraceful infirmity as long as he lives.

The problem we have whenever we face our spiritual duties is that they are holy and, except in a small degree, we are not. Consequently we have a wall of apathy to climb over before we can bring ourselves to do what belongs to the kingdom of God. The more honest with ourselves we are, the more we shall see this in ourselves and admit it. The New England Puritan Thomas Shepard confessed that often he would rather die than pray. Is it not so with us all? Praying, preaching, hearing sermons, keeping holy the Lord's Day, preparing for the Lord's Supper, visiting the sick and the dying with profitable conversation – all these things are inexplicably difficult to our fallen human natures. Men find it easier by far to opt rather for the church choir or the church social evening.

But it is just here that our soul is either made or else marred. If we are to rise above the dreadful mediocrity which prevails and which goes by the name of the normal Christian life, we must act on a new principle in the things we opt to do.

Among the first rules we need in order to deal with our deadness is this. We must school ourselves to do as a routine those things which are best for our souls. These duties are easy to recognise. They are invariably the things which we find hardest to do and from which we most recoil: the hearing of awakening preaching, the cultivation of the most spiritual persons as our bosom friends and acquaintance with God's presence by secret communion.

2. Do we feel most concern for what most concerns God?

There are Christians who, alas, give the impression of themselves that they are 'little men'. They have faith no doubt, but they are evidently interested in only that tiny fragment of God's cause which concerns themselves and in which they themselves play a part. They are large fish in a small pond. With the wider ocean of divine affairs they have little to do and they are in some cases jealous of their place and position within the sphere of their service.

The danger of such parochialism is that it has a very weak resistance to the virus of complacency. In process of time it generally results in a small-church mentality whose conceit is to fancy itself better than others, whoever the others may be. This is a pity and it is a great loss. It is deadness coming into the soul unobserved and on tiptoe.

It is no bad thing for us to cast about in our minds and to consider where God is most at work. God is not most where men suppose. His sovereign pleasure is to work in ways past finding out. But his presence is always to be detected by certain marks.

God is to be found in that church and in that society where there is most holy talk, most sense of sin, most tears of repentance, most dependence on Christ and most secret prayer. Conversely, God is least present in those churches where there is most vainglory, most worldliness, most carnal confidence, most contempt of others and most ecclesiastical bombast or pomposity.

It is another great rule for dealing with our deadness that we ought to love most those churches and persons where God most clearly is. The danger of all artificial church affiliations and denominations is that those who belong to them may love only those within their own group, or else love those of their own group best. But this leads to deadness if those of other groups and denominations are really more spiritual and more godly than those of our own. The antidote to complacency and decline is to love men, not because they 'belong to us' or are 'one of us' (as politicians speak) but because they are rich towards God. Much mischief follows when we love men in proportion to their loyalty to 'our cause' rather than to Jesus Christ's. Great is our deadness when we love those who pronounce our shibboleths and when we shun those who challenge our prejudices or else expose our complacency!

There is no dealing with the deadness of others till we start to deal with our own. And there is no dealing with the deadness of churches till we deal with the deadness of our own souls. When the axe of repentance is laid to the root of our natural self-love, we shall be at the place where we may expect to see God's gracious visitation to help us both at the personal and at the church level. But the task is no easy one if for no other reason than that deadness is intensely widespread and deep-seated. Moreover, few are apparently ready to deal with it as a matter of urgency.

13

The Remembrance of Old Sins

I t is of great importance to every believer that he should understand how to think of his own sins. Many of the mistakes which we make and miseries of mind which we suffer are closely connected to our ignorance about our present relation as Christians to our sins both past and present.

We assume that all well-instructed and experienced believers are agreed on the following points: that every sin, however small in our eyes, is most hateful to God; that the best actions of the best Christians are all defiled with sin; that sin in the Christian is still sin; that all the sins of a believer are pardoned for Christ's sake; and that a believer's lifelong duty is to strive towards unsinning perfection.

Putting these points another way, we may say that the following is our starting point as we review our relationship as Christians to our sins. First, sin in itself, in whomsoever it exists, is highly displeasing to God. Second, the best Christians have not in this life got beyond the commission of sin. Third, sin is not less sinful when committed by Christians. Fourth, no sins committed by a Christian can ever bring him into condemnation. Fifth, a Christian must not rest satisfied in his mere forgiveness but should daily strive after complete and sinless obedience to God, even though he knows it to be impossible in this life.

Proceeding from the above assumptions, we may consider our many-sided relationship to our sins in terms of the following headings:

1. The elect are no less sinful than others when God calls them to himself.

The habit of fallen minds is to slide continually into a spirit of self-righteousness. But, in order to cut away all glorying, God informs us that we 'were by nature children of wrath even as others' (*Eph.* 2:3) right up to the point of our conversion. It was not for our moral or spiritual superiority that God stooped down to save us, but out of his mere good pleasure and inexplicable grace.

It was as men and women who were 'in our blood' (*Ezek.* 16:6) that God saved us, by a gracious casting of the skirt of covenant mercy over our nakedness (*Ezek.* 16:8). As unregenerate and once-born sinners we were formerly, like all mankind, helplessly lost in our guilt and defilement. No difference of nature existed between the Christian, before his conversion, and the finally-impenitent sinner. So far as moral character is concerned, we were once 'even as others' (*Eph.* 2:3) who do not believe the gospel. There may have been a measure of respectability or decency. But even these blessings were the fruits of God's common goodness towards us. In our inward and true character we differed nothing from those who were already in hell. The elect began life as sinners who hated God and as men whose wills *could not* be obedient to God's will. Had not distinguishing love halted us in our tracks, we should most certainly have chosen that 'way which seemeth right unto a man' but whose end is 'death' (*Prov.* 16:25).

It is wholesome to the soul for believers to remember these dark facts about themselves. It is biblical to do so. We dare not go far along the pilgrim path without picturing to ourselves afresh this mortifying truth about ourselves. There was once a time in our life when we were 'afar off' (*Eph.* 2:17). We too were 'sometime alienated and enemies in our mind by wicked works' (*Col.* 1:21). Again and again the Apostle Paul pauses in the course of writing his Epistles to call his readers' attention to what they were before God's mercy changed them. Old sins should be remembered.

What advantages we should all have if we remembered our old sins oftener! Our love to God would be purer because our gratitude would be warmer. Our adoring praise for electing love would be more full and ardent than it is. We should get into mischief less often than we do. Our heads would hang lower with evangelical repentance and our talk would be more exclusively of a cross and of a Saviour.

Half the complaining and half the censoriousness which mars our lives as Christians would vanish if we called to mind more frequently the state in which we were born. We are therefore to practise often this exercise of soul: to tell ourselves that we are but 'brands plucked from the burning' (*Zech.* 3:2); coals taken from a fire in which others will burn eternally, pieces of sinful clay fit for the furnace of God's wrath till mercy saved us.

2. Though God will not judge a believer's sins in the sense of condemning him for them, yet God will in this life judge a believer's sins in the sense of chastening him for them.

There is no inconsistency in God's dealings with us as Christians. He has 'justified us freely by his grace' (*Rom.* 3:24). There is 'therefore now no condemnation' (*Rom.* 8:1).

Our past and present sins will, in a judicial sense, be 'remembered no more' (*Heb.* 8:12). He has 'cleansed us from all unrighteousness' (*1 John* 1:9).

However, the God who promises to pardon promises also to chasten his children. These two facts, so far from being at variance with one another, are both equally elements within the covenant arrangement which God has made for his people. These terms are stated most clearly in such a passage as Psalm 89:28–34:

> My mercy will I keep for him for evermore, and my covenant shall stand fast with him. His seed also will I make to endure for ever, and his throne as the days of heaven. If his children forsake my law, and walk not in my judgements; if they break my statutes, and keep not my commandments; Then will I visit their transgression with the rod, and their iniquity with stripes. Nevertheless my lovingkindness will I not utterly take from him, nor suffer my faithfulness to fail. My covenant will I not break, nor alter the thing that is gone out of my lips.

The Christian should live in a healthy fear of God's chastening. To have such fear is not to 'despise' God's chastening (*Heb.* 12:5). Rather, it is a part of the respect which he owes to God's holiness and love. God's chastisement, after all, is an expression of his anger. It is the anger of a Father, certainly, and not of a Judge. But it is anger nonetheless. No believer in his right mind can make light of God's chastisement, since he knows that God may take strong measures to correct his sins. We may smart for our evil behaviour in ways that we shall feel most keenly—perhaps all our life. Indeed, our sins may stir God to chasten us, not only in our own persons but in the persons of our children for generations after us.

Noah understood this when he prophetically cursed Canaan for centuries to come (*Gen.* 9:25). Eli's sins of omission as a parent were not the subject of a chastening which ended with his own death. The judgement was to carry forward to a generation still future and to children yet unborn. Eli's indulgent treatment of his wicked sons brought them to untimely deaths and made their posterity into beggars who for years to come must 'crouch . . . for a piece of silver and a morsel of bread' (*1 Sam.* 2:36). Similar lessons come to us from God's chastisements on Solomon and on Hezekiah (*1 Kings* 11:11; *Isa.* 39:7). And both were great men of God.

The message for us is plain. We are to rejoice in our free justification; but we must never presume to think that exemption from condemnation means exemption from chastisement. The only path of peace is the path of Christian obedience. If we are to enjoy peace there must first be holiness of life. Those who use justification as a pretext for sinning boldly must discover sooner or later that God will not long suffer sin in his own children. The Christian who angers God will never lose his soul, but he may lose more or less everything else.

It must be clearly seen from God's dealings with chastened saints in Scripture that sin is sin in the justified as well as in the unjustified. The believer, moreover, sins against God's love as well as against his justice. Our sins as believers are more sinful than others' sins in that wicked men, who have never enjoyed God's saving grace, cannot sin as we can against the love of a heavenly Father.

3. Though Christians have every right to believe that they are loved by God and fully pardoned, yet there remains a sense in which they must still hate themselves and mourn over their past and present sins.

It is a sign of great ignorance when a believer is at ease with his present state or at too great peace with himself. To have such an attitude is to be too healthy, and therefore to be unhealthy. The healthy believer is always suspicious of himself, always watchful over his own heart, always hungry for more holiness.

This attitude, which we here represent as healthy, must not be misinterpreted as morbidity or as lack of assurance. Evangelical assurance, when genuine, is sure of coming glory but also watchful over present temptation. Furthermore, evangelical assurance is entirely consistent with profound regret for past sin and awareness of present imperfection in oneself. Paul himself, whose assurance of salvation was strengthened by many supernatural favours, gifts and revelations, still felt it necessary to buffet his 'body and bring it into subjection lest, by any means, when he had preached to others, he himself should be a castaway' (*1 Cor.* 9:27). He feared the possibility of being finally lost and so took the requisite steps to protect his soul from so fearful a prospect.

Not only so, but the same apostle, though outstanding in holiness, still groaned under the felt impression of his own indwelling sin (*Rom.* 7:24). Also, he took with him to his dying day a sad recollection of the sins he had committed against Christ before his conversion (*Gal.* 1:13; *1 Cor.* 15:9; *1 Tim.* 1:13). His estimate of himself, arising from his grief for the way he had once persecuted the church, was that he was the least of the apostles and unfit even to bear the title of an apostle (*1 Cor.* 15:9).

From the above attitudes of Paul we may learn that it is good for the believer to carry with him a gospel sorrow for the sins which he has committed in the course of life—not only for sins done after conversion, but also for the 'old sins' (*2 Pet.* 1:9) of his unregenerate days. Such gospel sorrow does not consist of inconsolable anxiety or despair. It is not that haunting fear of divine vengeance which Paul may refer to as the 'spirit of bondage again to fear' (*Rom.* 8:15). Still less is it an obsessive or pathological sense of guilt found in some sad persons who are emotional cripples. Evangelical sorrow is a due sense of grief in a believer's soul arising out of his consciousness of having offended the God whom he supremely loves.

It is our conviction that such sorrow of soul is a sign of spiritual health. It is one element in the experience of a Christian which he must expect to have. Paul clearly had it. Augustine had it. The Reformers and Puritans knew and felt it; and so did the best of our evangelical forefathers. But, as far as the eye can see, this felt sense of sin is comparatively rare today. We no longer grieve over what we *are*. We no longer weep to think that we are corrupt in heart and blemished in character. Tragically, believers speak of human depravity as if it were a mere point of theology and not also a felt infirmity. Sin, if it is confessed at all, is confessed with careless formalism. A visitor from another world, if he attended our modern prayer meetings, might be pardoned for thinking that sin is only a religious term for an evil which believers talk about, but do not personally *experience*.

Old sins are of use to teach us new lessons. Old sins are often a photofit picture of our present spiritual deficiencies. Old sins are an index to unobserved infirmities. He who would be familiar with tomorrow's temptations, let him consider well yesterday's shortcomings. Every man, like the weather, has his own prevailing wind of susceptibility and will blow soonest towards his besetting sin. When grace is low in the soul the tide of our corruptions will carry us out towards the same old jagged rocks as they did in the past.

If to be forewarned is to be forearmed. Let us remember our old sins.

14

The Christian's Semi-Perfect State

There are few things in this life which can be said to be perfect. All the physicians in the world cannot make us perfectly healthy. All the cosmetics in the world cannot make us perfectly beautiful. All the books in the world cannot make us perfectly wise. All the churches in the world cannot make us perfectly good. We live among a ruined race and we learn to expect nothing but imperfection all the days we are here in this life. 'That which is crooked cannot be made straight and that which is wanting cannot be numbered.' So the Word of God informs us (*Eccl.* 1:15).

But what is not to be found in this world is to be found in the kingdom of God even here in this life. There are perfections to be had in the invisible kingdom of the saints even before they reach their eternal home above. It is our mistake to think that we can never have any form of perfection till we have left this world behind. It is good for us to make an inventory of present perfections.

First, the Christian's *pardon* is perfect. It is not merely that our sins before baptism are pardoned, or our sins before we take church membership. It is not the case that only our *past* sins are forgiven and no more. *All* sin and blasphemy is forgiven to those who are in Christ. Our future sins are as much forgiven as our sins of the past and present. They are 'cast into the depths of the sea' (*Mic.* 7:19), 'blotted out as a thick cloud' (*Isa.* 44:22), removed from us 'as far as the east is from the west' (*Psa.* 103:12).

Our pardon is already perfect. It admits of neither increase nor improvement. We shall not be more pardoned even in heaven itself, nor will our sins be any more blotted out when ten thousand years of glory are behind us. Pardon is perfect to all who believe in the crucified Saviour. If one half or one quarter of a sin remained unpardoned it could be enough to damn us forever. But this will never be. 'Their sins and their iniquities will I remember no more' (*Heb.* 8:12).

Secondly, our *new birth* is already perfect. It is understandable that many preachers might hesitate to say to believers that their *future* sins are pardoned before they are committed. Will that not lead to licence and to loose living? Will this doctrine not lead to a careless style of life? It *would* do, if it were not that pardon is never given to any except to those who have a new birth, and the new birth is a perfect thing. It alters our outlook and our attitude radically. It writes the law of God upon the tables of our heart. It inclines the will towards holy obedience. It fills the heart and soul with love to God.

It is true that the new birth does not make the believer perfect. Yet it is itself a perfect act of God which never needs to be repeated. If the new birth were not perfect we should need to be 'born again' again – and again, many times. But this is not so. The act of power which alters the soul and gives it a new love for God so changes us that we are a 'new creation' (*2 Cor.* 5:17). What was not there before is now present: a heart to love Christ, a tender conscience, a delight in new obedience.

Then again, *justification* is perfect in the believer. The man who is in Christ is as justified now as he will be in glory. Justification must needs be perfect or else it is nothing. A 'whole Christ' is ours now. His entire righteousness is ours now. The seamless garment of salvation is adequate to cloak and cover us fully in the sight of God. The believer is already 'legally perfect', if we may use the expression.

The claims of God's justice are wholly and entirely met by the provisions of his righteousness. What the law demands, the gospel provides. The righteousness exhibited in the gospel of our blessed Saviour Jesus Christ is the exact counterpart of all that the stringent demands of God's law and justice could ever require from us as his creatures. To believe in Jesus is to 'honour the law' and to 'establish' it (*Rom.* 3:31) perfectly. So rich is God in his goodness to all who come to him by the gospel way. The finishing touches were put to our justification when our bleeding Surety cried, 'It is finished' and when he rose from the dead. Let those who understand drink in deeply from this word of comfort: 'We are the righteousness of God in him' (*2 Cor.* 5:21).

Closely related to this is the fact that believers are the beneficiaries of a perfect *atonement*. The blood of our Lord and Saviour is perfectly, eternally and in every way acceptable to the Heavenly Father. The cross is the central glory of history and of the whole universe. All angels marvel at its sublime perfection. All saints, whether below or above, adore God for it. Christ stooped to conquer, bore in his soul the lightning of eternal vengeance, quenched the full fury of an offended God, in love for us was made sin and melted the frown of heaven into a smile of favour. Nothing in history matches the height of glory which Jesus' sufferings accomplished. The cross is the crown of all God's works, the pinnacle of his wisdom and the acme of his love. The atonement possesses a perfection which beggars language itself, and it possesses that perfection *now* as it works blessing and peace in our lives.

The believer's *adoption* is perfect in this life: 'Beloved, now are we the sons of God' (*1 John* 3:2). John here admits that 'it doth not yet appear what we shall be' (*1 John* 3:2), but he affirms that we shall not be in glory any more the sons of God than we already are. Whatever glories await us at the last day, they will not improve on the fact of our adoption, for this fact is a fact now. It is of course true that our *enjoyment* of our adoption will greatly increase in the last day. The privileges and favours of our adopted condition will vastly increase when our Lord himself appears on the clouds to call us home to glory. But the Christian is as much a son of God in his present state of humiliation as ever he will be in his resurrected and heavenly state. We are sons of God *now*. That is a clear fact of revelation and one which must stir within every Christian the warm feelings of deep gratitude to God.

We are speaking just now of the perfections of this present life. It is well for us to do so. We are apt to fall into bad habits of thought and to resign ourselves unthinkingly to the feeling that in this life 'nothing is perfect'. This is not true and we must not let our unthinking minds convince us that it is so. In this imperfect world there are perfect things within the Christian, and a perfect Book too in his hand.

However, when all this is said, there are imperfections also in the believer. We are as yet in a state of grace; and grace is not glory. Grace makes us good, but not perfectly good. In glory we shall be good and nothing but good. In glory we shall be better than Adam on the day of his creation. He was perfect but able to sin; we shall be perfect and unable to sin.

The believer's present state is therefore an unfinished one. The believer is presently undergoing a process. He is on his way to future perfection. As yet the process is incomplete. But it is going to be completed. Our struggles against sin within and sin without are evidences of the fact that we do not sin with our whole will, as unsaved sinners do. If we could, we would never sin again. Our wish is to be perfect now. But our wish is beyond our strength. Two laws are presently at work within us. The law of sin and the law of grace are in constant collision both in our inward consciousness and in our outward performance. The inward failure is painful to us; and this failure, when it becomes outward and visible, is mortifying. But all such failure on the believer's part is but for a time. Our victory is at hand, and it is sure. The 'legal perfection' which is our present justified state, will assuredly be matched at length, after we have 'suffered a little while' (*1 Pet.* 5:10) by a perfect sanctification also.

It is a comfort to us as Christians to remember that we are already in a half-perfect condition. The enemy of our souls is good at his work of demoralising us with his half-truths: 'You are still a sinner.' Yes, but a sinner saved and on the way to heaven. 'You are no better than others.' I deserve what all sinners will receive, but I have a Saviour who died for me and my standing before God is in a perfect righteousness. 'You are very far from perfect.' I am only as far from perfection as the day of my death, which may, in God's good will, be very near.

Though we appear very much like others we are very far different from them in the judgement of heaven. One half of our redemption is true of us already: justified, covered by atoning blood, adopted, born from above, 'heirs of God and joint heirs with Christ' (*Rom.* 8:17). We are, if you will, half-made saints in this present life. Part of the process of perfecting us is past, part remains to be done. Let no Christian suppose that he is no better now than when he had no grace. Just because we are not yet at home is no argument to say that we are not well on the way there.

What then are the imperfect aspects of the Christian in this life? The most serious and in need of our attention are not our imperfect happiness and our imperfect comfort. Far more serious are our spiritual and moral imperfections. These are what demand our daily study and our reforming zeal.

Our first imperfection lies in our imperfect *faith*. Faith is the root of all our graces, and needs our priority attention. We do not believe God's Word as we should. From this spring a thousand seeds of evil. Unbelief is the daisy and dandelion of the soul. It ruins the lawns, the flowerbeds, the paths and all else. Hence our Saviour so frequently chides his people with this as their besetting weakness: 'O ye of little faith.' Let us believe every word of God, every doctrine, every promise, every threatening, every law – let us live like those who take God's every word for truth, and so stake our life, soul, eternity and all on the word which he has said. God's word can no more fail than the waters could fail from the sea, or the sun cease to rise each day, 'Heaven and earth shall pass away: but my words shall not pass away' (*Mark* 13:31).

Another imperfection in the Christian is his *conversion*. We are not turned to God yet as perfectly as we need to be and ought to be. The new birth is complete at once. But our conversion is ongoing. We need to convert to God more and more each day and in every way. Let us turn to God more in prayer, in submission, in repentance, in love, in delight, in praise, in service and in expectation of his blessing. What distinguishes a Rutherford, a M'Cheyne or a Brainerd from most other Christians but that these men were more perfectly turned to God in heart and life? May God increasingly turn us all.

The imperfection which burdens the believer most in this life is his imperfect *sanctification*. The standard of perfection is the moral law. This standard was reached only once in history, when our Lord and Saviour lived loving God with all his soul and his neighbours as himself. To others it is the least of their worries that they do not keep God's law; to the Christian it is the greatest. It is hard to pardon ourselves that we love God so little; that we bless God with the tongue at one moment and speak sharply of our neighbour with it the next; that we think so many unworthy thoughts; that we do so little to benefit mankind with the gospel; that we advance so slowly in the knowledge of God's Word.

But the 'Woe is me!' in the Christian's heart is a mark of grace and a sure sign that, though not yet perfect, he is already half-perfect. The grace we have is all the gift of God and one of the blessings of grace is that we see our need of more. It is the purpose of God to give us more till we reach that happy land where grace, like the manna, will cease and we shall *eat* the good fruit of the land forever.

15

The Christian and His Fears

I f the devil cannot stop our progress towards heaven he can, and will, attempt to hinder it. Among the various weapons used by Satan to slacken our pace is that of fear. We must remember that the devil knows the Bible better than we do and has been a diligent student of it since it was first written. His motive in studying the Bible cannot be to prevent the fulfilment of God's promises or prophecies. This he knows he cannot do. But in order to search out ways to dampen *our* confidence in these promises of God and thereby to weaken our hands and impede our progress. If Satan cannot stop the elect from reaching home he will at least make their journey uncomfortable for them. And few things are more uncomfortable than living under a cloud of fear.

As Christians we must never underestimate the importance of morale. Our states of mind have a great influence on our entire life and witness, either for better or for worse. Joy unites all the faculties of the soul and makes us run in the way of obedience and service to God. But heaviness in the heart causes it to stoop, to falter and to hang down. Once we lose our joy we lose our momentum, just as a motor vehicle loses its 'revs'. The hills then become difficult to climb and the machinery of the soul grates and vibrates with strain. Every fresh task is a burden almost too heavy to bear. Every new challenge appears to be edged and tinted with darkness. To the joyless soul every duty is only a drudge.

The devil, as a master of psychology, is expert at darkening the aspect of our lives with gloom and thereby sapping the joy out of our soul. The things of God always tend to inspire us, to lift up our hearts, to restore our assurance. But the devices of Satan have exactly the opposite effect. They are calculated to darken and depress, to intimidate and discourage. Satan aims to make *us* inefficient, to wear us out with anxiety, to divert our energies by morbid introspection from joyful service for Christ to hopeless inactivity . . . and even to despair.

Much of this mischief our great enemy is able to bring about by means of fear. This fear comes over the soul mysteriously and at first almost imperceptibly; yet it comes like thick clouds over the soul till there is hardly light enough to see any of God's promises clearly. Fear covers the mind like fog over the landscape. It shuts out the sun and closes in our visibility. It also brings with it some degree or other of misery and robs us of our delight in God.

It is the Christian's great art to combat his fears and to render them impotent. This he is to do by 'acting faith' – the expression is old-fashioned but good– in the Word of God. That is to say, the Christian is to be alert to the approach of darkness, discouragement and fear within his own mind. He is to have at the ready ways and means of repelling those thoughts which threaten to pull down the curtain of fear upon his spirit. Just as the prudent householder has always on hand a fire extinguisher, so the well-armed believer has means within reach to extinguish his fears and to dampen the squibs thrown into his mind by the evil one.

Let no one imagine that this is an easy thing to do. The utterances of inspired saints in the Bible make it very clear that not one of them found it an easy exercise to repel the fears and doubts which came upon them. The Books of Psalms and of Job, even if we had no others, tell us plainly that the greatest of God's people have had to wrestle against their fears with agony, with occasional failure and with experience of intense inward darkness. It is unlikely to be otherwise with us in our day.

The soul behaves sinfully when it looks at its perceived problems apart from the power of God. The fact that mankind has such fears at all is evidence that we are all born practical atheists. In one sense mankind's fears are a judgement from God upon us for our unbelief. The soul was made, like a wine glass, to be a vessel for something more important and more precious than itself. The soul was at the first created to be a 'receptacle' of the Holy Spirit. God originally *lived* in the soul of man as in a temple or sanctuary. He made man, in a peculiar and special way, for himself.

The day Adam sinned he died, not physically but spiritually. He lost the Spirit's gracious inhabitation and mankind became 'flesh'. No alteration could be more complete or more catastrophic. For man, who was at first made 'a living soul' (*Gen.* 2:7) to become 'flesh' was for him to become an empty vessel, devoid of that privilege of communion with his Maker for which his innermost being was specially designed.

A 'godless' man is an unnatural phenomenon. By the Fall man became what he was not created to be. Not without cause did the learned Augustine state: 'Thou hast made us for thyself and our heart is restless till it finds its rest in thee'. This restlessness can only cease when the eternal God re-enters the soul of man at the new birth and by so doing restores to it its integrity, happiness and comfort. This is what the gospel of our Lord and Saviour Jesus Christ does and which nothing else can do for us.

There are, of course, sinless fears as well as sinful ones. Such fears are to be seen in the life of our Saviour as he faced the experiences which would come upon him when he was made sin for us. There was no taint of sin in these fears of Christ. In all that he feared he had perfect love for his people and perfect trust in God. His holy soul was filled with the Spirit 'without measure' (*John* 3:34). The fears of Christ were all a rational and lawful recoil from the fiery flame of damnation which he did not deserve to suffer.

To state the matter in this way is not to pretend to explain all the mystery of fear or suffering which he underwent for us as the God-Man. But if we cannot explain fully how a perfect and divine person may have deep fears, we can, and must, veil our faces in awe and love. It is enough now to know that he entered into the dark arena of fear that we might be delivered from it finally and forever.

What more directly concerns us now is to learn how to fight against those fears which Satan brings into our souls because we are sinful. To this subject we turn in the hope of finding light and help. If we could but keep our souls free from sinful fears and cares we should lend speed to ourselves in the service of God here below. If we could be 'careful for nothing' (*Phil.* 4:6), according to the teaching of the Bible, we should know very much more of the joy of the Lord (*Phil.* 4:4). Which Christian can doubt that this would add greatly to his comfort and usefulness in the present life?

If, as we have affirmed, our sinful fears arise when we look at our problems apart from God, it must follow that our line of self-defence is to view our problems always in the context of God's power. This is an art which we shall spend a whole lifetime learning and re-learning. For this reason we are told that 'man doth not live by bread only but by every word of God' (*Deut.* 8:3). Bread is for the body, which is the lesser part of man. But the soul needs spiritual light and knowledge and this can come only from holy Scripture.

Those who do not read the Bible or go to churches where the Bible is explained and expounded have no effective means for warding off their fears. This is the tragedy of our modern 'post-Christian' society. It has shaken off the fear of God but is a prey to every other kind of fear. For this is the law of God's just providence, that those who fear God should have nothing else to fear; but those who do not fear God must become slaves to a thousand fears.

The Christian is therefore happy in this, that he has the Word of God beside him, in his mouth and in his heart. In this blessed Word he has the means of countering all the suggestions of Satan. The art he is to learn is the practical wisdom of how to apply his knowledge of God's Word to the encounters which he has with the devil.

Satan seeks to take advantage of us by presenting to our mind the problems we face in a false light. He is the 'father of lies' (*John* 8:44) in that he represents to our minds difficulties and problems which he makes out at the moment to be inescapably menacing. By a combination of bullying and misrepresentation he drives our soul into a mood of darkness. His whispered taunts are: 'There is no way out of this problem', 'There is no comfort now', 'There is a catastrophe ahead', and so on.

If we allow Satan to persuade us that his arguments are sound, we shall not be able to save ourselves from bouts of semi-despair and gloom. The skilful believer, when he senses his spirit to be under satanic attack, must be up and about with his knowledge of the Bible to remind himself that there is no situation at all from which an almighty God and Father cannot save him.

How Satan's lies are so persuasive is a mystery. He must have given to him some power which he is able to use with tremendous effect upon our soul. As the viper strikes and the scorpion bites so that the venom spreads through the whole body bringing rapid death, so does Satan have some wounding power over our human souls.

Almost one half of a Christian's fears arise from anxiety about yesterday's troubles. The other half arise from our anxiety about tomorrow. Seldom do we have anxiety about what we experience *now*. To repel our fears therefore we must try to live by faith in the here-and-now of our life. The past we cannot alter; the future may never happen as we imagine. If we are to know peace we shall need to trust in God with the certainty that he is working 'all things perfectly' for us (*Psa.* 57:2).

The devil's art is to get us to live by sight and not by faith. The story of the twelve spies in the book of Numbers is a perfect illustration of this (chapter 14). The way in which the believing spies viewed the land was the exact reverse of the others. The difference lay in their attitude, and their attitude was governed by their faith, or lack of it. So it is with us in all aspects of our life in this world.

The golden rule is that we must refuse to view anything in our life in isolation from the promises of God's Word. So much of what we hear and read and see in the 'News' inevitably is presented to us from the perspective of atheistic unbelief. Hence it comes with the sting of fear. It weakens, discourages, hurts. Today probably as never before in history 'men's hearts fail them for fear' (*Luke* 21:26). No wonder, if they sadly ignore what God has said.

We who believe that history, destiny and all else belong to God must seek to live above this spirit of fear for 'God has not given us the spirit of fear; but of power, and of love, and of a sound mind' (*2 Tim.* 1:7). To do so will be an invaluable benefit to our spiritual life.

16

A Psalm from the Cave: Psalm 142

The title of Psalm 142 informs us that this portion of God's Word was written by David 'when he was in the cave'. Every Bible reader remembers at once that this cave of Adullam was the headquarters of David during that early and very difficult part of his life when he was being persecuted by King Saul.

There were no doubt many respects in which David's life in the cave of Adullam was uncomfortable and irksome to him. A cave is a gloomy home at best, lit by only a tiny fragment of natural light and never cheered, even in summer, by warmth or fresh air. But this cave was ordained by God's providence to be the place where David was to be fitted for his kingdom. 'Before honour is humility' (*Prov.* 15:33) and David, type of Christ that he was, had to stoop very low before he was set upon his regal throne. The believer must not become impatient with God's discipline in this life. We need our seasons of humiliation. There are great lessons to be learnt in the cave, as this Psalm will show.

One may suppose that the companions of David were a daily trial to his spirit in the cave. It is true that he had there the congenial companionship for a while of 'his brethren and all his father's house' (*1 Sam.* 22:1). Yet this must have been much offset by the character and by the large number of those malcontents who had fled to the cave to find asylum with him there: 'everyone that was in distress, and everyone that was in debt, and everyone that was discontented, gathered themselves unto him . . . about four hundred men' (*1 Sam.* 22:2).

Amid debt-ridden and malcontented men, then, David learned to wait on God. Here was the seminary in which he had his tuition in godliness. Here too, as this Psalm shows us, David was taught to sing the songs of Zion, songs which would be sung and re-sung as long as the militant church of Christ would be on earth. The Christian who cannot go to any school of theology may, if he is teachable, learn inspiring lessons under God, even in the dark places of this world. There is honey for Christians in the cave.

It requires no stretching of the imagination to realise that David must often have longed for the day when he could quit the cave of Adullam and take up his rightful place on the throne of Israel and Judah. It was a sore trial to his spirit to be unjustly hounded by Saul. No just and upright man enjoys being treated like a scoundrel. David had vivid recollections of the spear hurled at him by Saul and which had narrowly missed his head (*1 Sam.* 19:10). He had fled in fear repeatedly from the presence of Saul. He could recall the time when, to save his own life, he had feigned madness at the court of Achish (*1 Sam.* 21:10–15). He could think back to the painful day when news came to him that Saul had murdered all the priests at Nob save one (*1 Sam.* 22:9–23). No wonder David's spirit often sighed, 'How long, O Lord, how long?' (*Psa.* 13:1; 94:3,4). God will teach his people to be patient with the wicked as he himself is patient. There is a needful process of sanctification going on inside every Christian who is in the cave.

We shall not surely err when we suppose that David must often have wondered at the seeming slowness of God's promises, while he lived in the cave. David's certainty of being king rested on the Word of God. His warrant to expect his kingdom sprang from the Lord's command to Samuel: 'Fill thy horn with oil . . . I will send thee to Jesse the Bethlehemite: for I have provided me a king among his sons' (*1 Sam.* 16:1); and when David stood before Samuel, the old prophet was told: 'Arise, anoint him: for this is he' (*1 Sam.* 16:12). Moreover, 'the Spirit of the Lord came upon David from that day forward' (*1 Sam.* 16:13). Both Word and Spirit assured David that his title to the throne was good. But long, weary years were to pass before God's promise would be fulfilled. The believer has a good title to possess heaven as his home and the earth as his inheritance (*John* 14:3; *Matt.* 5:5). But God's promises are not fulfilled till we have 'suffered a while' (*1 Pet.* 5:10). It is needful for the believer to have his faith and patience tried. Heaven becomes ever more precious to those who are in the cave.

It is with no small degree of awe and wonder that we have frequently read about those good saints of old who, among many other sufferings and privations 'wandered in deserts, and in mountains, and in dens and caves of the earth' (*Heb.* 11:38). If we ever stopped to ask ourselves what they did in their solitude or in their sorrow we find a practical answer in the Psalm to which we have turned. They lifted up their eyes, as many a Waldensian, Covenanter and Huguenot was to do in after days, to the God of all hope. They 'endured as seeing him who is invisible'; they 'looked for a city which hath foundations, whose builder and maker is God' (*Heb.* 11:10).

We do not naturally love to live as exiles on the earth. But it is good for the soul because it gives to us a true perspective on this life. When we are lulled in the lap of pleasure we see God as small and earth as great. Our love for God declines; our appetite for worldly delights grows stronger. But when we are tossed to and fro in the earth and 'emptied from vessel to vessel' (*Jer.* 48:11) we recognise the world to be the nothing that it is; we then see God to be our great and only good.

This was David's experience as he wrote the Psalm which we are considering:

I cried unto the Lord with my voice; with my voice unto the Lord did I make my supplication (v.1).

The pressure of his thoughts was so great that he could not rest content, as often we all do, with silent prayer. Anguish and deep feeling pressed on him so heavily that he could find relief only in loud cries to God. How true it is that prayer is born out of need! The sharper our sense of need, the warmer and louder our cry to God will be. Our experiences of the cross in everyday life are ordained to make us cry out to our loving Father in heaven, even as our Saviour's experience of the cross constrained him to 'offer up prayers and supplications with strong crying and tears' to his Father in heaven (*Heb.* 5:7).

Are we sore pressed in this life? Let not the Christian seek relief in cheap music or entertainment. Let him get good out of his miseries by going to his God in secret. There let him cry out aloud to him who hears the groaning cry and rewards his people openly. Weakness in prayer results when the believer escapes into the arms of this world's entertainers. To God let us raise our voice.

I poured out my complaint before him; I shewed before him my trouble (v.2).

Trouble loosens the tongue. We are sometimes tongue-tied before God. Our powers of utterance are feeble and our pitiful trickle of thought is soon dried up. But life in the 'cave' of God's discipline will teach us again how to pray. Here David's prayers and plaintive petitions pour forth in a torrent. We may not complain against God; but we may pour out our complaints into his ears. Like Hezekiah, he spreads forth his needs before the Almighty. He tells us this to teach us to imitate him: 'I shewed before him my trouble'.

That is why God brings us as his people into trouble. It is so that we may, in turn, show it to God. In so doing we get a double benefit. We exercise our faith in God's power to deliver us; and we leave our cares and burdens at his door.

When my spirit was overwhelmed within me, then thou knewest my path. In the way wherein I walked have they privily laid a snare for me (v.3).

Here David tells us the substance of his prayer. He makes a digest of the things which he said to God. He was not ashamed to admit his inward feelings to have been very difficult to bear. It is hard to be 'overwhelmed' in our minds. Circumstances can be so trying that we feel swamped by them. We feel as though we are to drown in a sea of troubles. But even when circumstances are at their worst, God 'knows our path'. By faith we see that we are not deserted when we feel most deserted. The Christian is surrounded by God's holy watchers who attend us, all unnoticed, on our dangerous path.

But the believer's path is beset with unseen snares. Ecumenical voices whisper and beckon him into the 'wider church' with its easier creeds and lifestyle. Well-disguised errors catch at his heels to ensnare him and to inoculate him against serious religion by their lies and by their lightness. There are a thousand places which are out of bounds to God's people in this life. The halls and clubs of vice are good news to the thoughtless, but the Lord's people recognise that they are snares.

I looked on my right hand, and beheld, but there was no man that would know me: refuge failed me; no man cared for my soul (v.4).

There is loneliness and loneliness. What David here feels is *spiritual* loneliness, which is more severe than natural loneliness. Those who suffer natural loneliness suffer because they have no friends near them. But those who have the experience of spiritual loneliness are lonely because men *will* not befriend them. They are rejected and shunned because they are *God's* people, whom others regard as 'too serious' and 'too religious'. The light of heaven is in their eye and so men prefer not to associate with them. This may happen to a child of God in his own family . . . in his own home . . . in his own *church*!

This spiritual loneliness is further expressed in this, that David had no man to 'care for his soul'. When we have a fellow believer at hand we have a place of 'refuge'. But refuge fails us when we have no sympathetic Christian with whom to share the concerns of our souls. There was no Jonathan at hand to tell his sorrow to.

Many a Christian has been in this lonely 'cave' when 'no man cares for his soul'. Let us value our times of fellowship and not waste them. Let us care for the souls of our brethren in every way we can.

I cried unto thee, O Lord: I said, Thou art my refuge and my portion in the land of the living (v.5).

David, who a moment ago found no refuge, now tells us that he has found a refuge at last. It is in *God*. Do we realise that God is the believer's sanctuary when all else fails? All creature comforts are but a pale shadow of the fulness and sufficiency which we have in God in the worst of times.

When our life in this world's dreary 'cave' seems to be shorn of all comfort and all joy, we have another world to turn to. God himself is a world of joy to the lonely soul that draws near to him by faith. Luther would say so and he would point to his time of trial at Worms. Rutherford would say so and point to his confinement at Aberdeen. Many a modern saint would say the same today in Turkey or in some Arab land where darkness and the frequent call to prayer from the nearby mosque reminds him that he is a stranger here on earth. 'Whom have I in heaven but thee? and there is none upon earth that I desire beside thee' (*Psa.* 73:25). Let us make God our refuge from the noisy clamour of our modern world. The whole world will one day be hushed in silence forever. The believer's life is scarcely yet begun. Our time of greatest joy is to be when time itself is over.

Attend unto my cry; for I am brought very low: deliver me from my persecutors; for they are stronger than I (v.6).

It is mortifying to the Christian when he feels that God is not listening to his prayers. As a child pulls at its mother's sleeve to draw her attention, so does a believer importune God till He attends to his prayers and sends a comforting blessing. This is all the more true when we are conscious of being surrounded by those who hate us for our love of God. David calls them 'persecutors' and such they certainly are. They dislike what we stand for and they are very often stronger than we are.

It is the wonder of the ages that the weak and timid church of Jesus Christ has survived all the hordes of persecutors who have attempted to exterminate her all through history. There are many doing so still at this very hour. They would gladly silence the voice of the gospel and exile truth to another world, if they could. But God is the hidden strength of his people in all ages. The strength of men is greater than the church; but the 'weakness of God is stronger than men'.

However discouraged we are, we must not dream foolish dreams. The church will never be destroyed in the earth. All the church's enemies at last have had to leave their task unfinished. So Julian the Apostate's last words tell us: 'Thou hast conquered, O Galilean!'. Jesus and his church rose up on the waves of providence, while the proud empire of Rome sank down forever.

Bring my soul out of prison, that I may praise thy name: the righteous shall compass me about; for thou shalt deal bountifully with me (v.7).

David's soul, like his body, was in a 'prison'. The cave of Adullam must often have closed in upon his spirits and made him feel oppressed. But his faith and hope look forward to the good which God will do him in a coming day: 'The righteous shall compass me about; for thou shalt deal bountifully with me'. God would one day take him out of this cave and set him on the throne of his people. Then there would be loud shouts from all good men: 'God save the King'. There was to be a coronation day, a time of festivity. The ark would be carried at last to Zion. The tabernacle would become a temple. Yea, more! In the course of time, another 'David' would come who would sit at God's right hand in the glory above. Sin would be one day atoned for forever.

Sinners would cease to be. Heaven and earth would pass away. The trumpet would sound and the new world appear in which there dwells righteousness.

Let us be of good cheer. David's prayerful meditation is more than half fulfilled. Time itself is in short supply. Soon we shall see a Saviour coming down to take us home. There will be no more 'cave' then!

17

Why Is There No Wrestling?

It is a question worth pondering as to whether there is much serious prayer being offered up in our busy age. There is undoubtedly a welter of other things being attempted: files of paper are prepared on a host of topics; memoranda by the score are recorded; statistics are noted; committees are formed and then disbanded; agendas are drawn up and discussed; ideas are floated and debated; proposals are offered and turned this way and then that. But in the face of the massive onslaught of secular and spiritual forces hostile to the gospel of Christ there appears to be little agonising prayer. Perhaps it is time to ask ourselves if this is why nothing seems to get any better.

Behind this lack of real prayer – if the above observations are just – there would appear to lie just one basic explanation: prayer is extraordinarily difficult. At least prayer which involves wrestling is so. There is a common style of praying found in many places today which makes but little demand upon those who offer it up. We do not set ourselves up to be the judges of other men's spirituality. But if our eyes and ears do not deceive us it would seem that a style of prayer is widespread which consists very much of saying thank you to God for a large number of things, yet never goes on to lay hold of the Almighty or to make massive demands upon his promises.

It is time to ask ourselves whether such praying is worthy of being called scriptural or evangelical. The prayers of the Bible concentrate on the great emergency and crisis of the times. Examples of this abound. The prayers of Ezra, Nehemiah and Daniel may be taken as notable examples. They grapple with the main issue of the day, which is that God should pardon his people and restore to them the power of his grace. No doubt these holy men were grateful to God for the mercies of life and thanked him no less than we do today. But their chief energies in prayer were spent, not in reference to the common mercies of life, but on those themes and subjects which most concerned Christ's kingdom at that hour. So they contain the element of striving with God. They are hot and passionate. They amount to a spiritual wrestling and to a laying hold of God in downright earnest.

If anyone thinks that we go too far in so speaking of prayer in Bible times, let him recall the marvellous earnestness recorded for us concerning the prayers of our Lord in the garden. How deeply did he experience agony! There was immense conflict in his mind and soul. This was registered in his tears and in his sweat which dripped from his brow like clots of blood. Such intensity of prayer may perhaps be unique to our blessed Redeemer. But there are expressions elsewhere in the Bible to show that prayer is hard and demanding to man.

The Psalmist speaks of an experience which must be exceeding rare in our times. His knees were weak through fasting (*Psa.* 109:24). Intercessory prayer requires us to 'afflict our souls' (*Lev.* 16), to 'watch' and not to sleep (*Matt.* 26:38), to 'labour fervently' (*Col.* 4:12), to persevere (*Eph.* 6:18) and to engage in an exercise which is intensely spiritual (*Rom.* 8:26).

When we study the practice of Old Testament saints we find not a little to humble and inspire us. Elijah's prayers stopped heaven and brought a drought on the land. Again, his prayers opened heaven and poured forth rain on the parched earth. What prayers these biblical men and women offered up and with what effect upon the world! They stormed Zion in their fervour to be heard. They petitioned the throne of heaven and laid siege to its walls. They would scarcely take No for an answer. In so praying they stopped the sun in its course; they called down fire from above; they opened prisons; they overturned the schemes of armies; they raised the dead; they toppled thrones; they wrought mighty deeds of victory.

It cannot escape our attention that such wrestlers with God seem to be few today. We are grateful for those who serve Christ in whatever capacity. We value highly all who walk with God and are true to his Word and sound in their faith. But it would be good for our land and for our churches if there were a larger army of wrestlers, all taking God at his Word and pleading relentlessly the promises which he has made to his people in a dark day. In a word, we need an army of men and women who are so devoted to praying for the Spirit to come down that they give God no rest (*Isa.* 62:7).

Too many prayers lack steam. Too many prayers are predictable. Too many prayers are marked by sameness and tameness. But prayers which are ordinary are not sufficient to turn the tide of evil in these days. What is called for in such a dark day is for men and women of exceptional dedication to God who will plead for a mighty change in the state of things. Perhaps this is the main reason why there has been a recovery of much truth but little public manifestation of it. We are all guilty in that we have not waited with sufficient seriousness on God to give the church the power of preaching and the unction of spiritual energy.

It is a fault to treat prayer as the Cinderella of our spiritual duties. To read and to preach is essential. But the oil of divine blessing must needs be poured on the means of grace if they are to be effectual. Too many of our services to Christ are performed with little water on the mill. It is the way of God that he will have us beg for our blessings. Little prayer usually means little unction. There are exceptions but we must not take advantage of God's kindness. At times we get unusual help in our work with but little intercession beforehand. But it is presumptuous of us to take this as our rule of action.

A common reason why we cease to pray effectually or fervently is because we fall into a rut. When this happens we pray more by habit than in the Spirit. We do indeed go through a routine of words and lists but the fire is just not there in the soul. This is one reason why we must be careful not to be dictated to by our prayer lists. They may have their place but they must never become our masters. At times – perhaps at frequent times – we must leave our prayer lists aside and turn from our conventional patterns of prayer. There are times when the mould of our intercession is to be discarded entirely and we are to devote our whole minds and souls to the great task of calling on God for nothing less than revival. Let the soul pour itself out to its Maker in anguished groans. Let the heart within us feel free to roam up and down the land in its search for a way to give vent to our burden and to our grief that Christ's cause is so low.

We shall probably seldom if ever pray in the manner of the saints of the Bible if we are not full of the knowledge of the Scriptures. This is clear from a perusal of the great prayers of the Bible itself. The Bible characters whom we referred to as great in prayer were themselves men who were full of Scripture. Their prayers are often a tissue of biblical language. They quote not only the ideas of the Bible but also its very text. Of course there is a danger even in this. It is possible to use the Bible as mere padding in our prayers. It is sometimes the case that men who have little to say in prayer fill out their prayers by reciting texts of Scripture which may be only partially what they are trying to say. We have all been guilty, no doubt. This is an abuse. Real prayer shoots upwards, being impelled by the inward fire and animation of the soul. No one needs to be told when we have offered up a real prayer. It is something which all feel who have any spiritual life in them.

However, it is to be feared that many cannot pray with fervour because they are simply ignorant of the Word of God. It is not simply a matter of which version we use. The point in hand is that whatever version men use they should know it through and through. We are to be full of the knowledge of God's Word, and we are to use it in prayer, not as a way of filling out and decorating our thoughts but as a way of pleading with God in terms of what he himself has said and thus of arguing before him the unchangeableness of his own holy promises in the light of our present needs.

It appears to be the case that, generally speaking, we are only as good in our public prayers as we are in our private devotions. The measure of the one will be the measure of the other. If anything, private prayer is more difficult. The reason for this is probably that there is more excitement of the soul where there is a gathering of God's people together. It is less exhilarating to pray on one's own. Moreover there is a special promise from Christ to those who gather in prayer: 'For where two or three are gathered together in my name, there am I in the midst of them' (*Matt.* 18:20). This is surely one part of the explanation as to why public prayer is easier. For this reason alone it is essential that the Christian, especially the Christian minister, should give attention to secret prayer. Here he will grow in holy boldness. Here he will learn the art of drawing near to God, an art which will make him robust in prayer when he has to stand in the assembly of the people.

But how is a man to *begin* in this work of learning to pray with passion? We are not wrong to think that this is something which we are to learn. For though it is true that all our powers of soul come as a gift from God, yet they are powers which we are to cultivate and to grow in. Some have a special gift in prayer. But all of us are to stir up ourselves to improve in this grace. 'Exercise thyself unto godliness' (*1 Tim.* 4:7). As the professional sportsman must train daily so must the man or woman of God train in spiritual gifts, and exercise the soul in holy duties. It is the royal way to excellence. And excellence in prayer is what our churches so much need in this time, surely.

The thing which we must start with if we are to begin to develop the soul in this wrestling type of prayer is time. It is impossible to pray in the way we are suggesting if we do not set apart time for this exercise. Some days we are so busy with legitimate calls on our time that we cannot pray in this specially urgent manner. But from time to time we must set aside the special hour for this sacred work. The believer must in that hour be away from the distractions of the telephone and of the other numerous interruptions which on other occasions we must be prepared for.

When this time is secured we need next to have our hearts brought to a glow of expectation. Emotion is one of the secrets of lively prayer. Whatever will fire the affections with heat and ardour is to be desired. In other words, we shall not pray as we ought at these times of special urgency until we have prepared ourselves. There is a preparation needed for the highest type of prayer. It consists of a rousing of our faith. It becomes a factor of our consciousness. It consists of a yearning desire to move God to bless us with help.

There are undoubtedly times when the Spirit creates a yearning desire for prayer when there has been no conscious preparation on our part. On such occasions we should yield to this impulse. Other duties can wait. When once the heart has become fired with a passion to hold communion with God, other things should be laid aside for the moment and the impulse to pray yielded to. This is so because this urge to pray is in itself so scarce in this world and so precious a gift from God that it should take precedence over other things. The result will normally be that we shall enjoy a time of ecstatic nearness with God. This is a taste of heaven on earth and is probably better for the soul than anything else whatever. There is no spiritual joy comparable to pouring out the heart in burdened intercession. Those who are acquainted with this exercise will know that it is a taste of glory. However, usually we need to prepare ourselves for prayer by meditation, singing or reading.

We need not be in a hurry in our special time of prayer. It is not necessary to rush at the main point to be prayed. Let the soul begin calmly. Let there be no attempt at generating false fire. All our desire at this early point is to have our hearts moistened. What should happen is that as we spend time in the presence of God the world falls away from our mind and we grow into the attitude of looking up in expectation. It is often, not always, a help to pray out loud to God. This is a good way of improving our concentration. We wish him to visit us with a shower of grace. Our yearning is that he should manifest himself to us not as to the world (*John* 17:6). This early part of prayer is certainly the hardest. Many give up at this early stage and stop their prayer before they have, as it were, begun.

What we wish to do is to bring before God the cause which he loves more than we do. We expostulate with him that he stands so aloof from his own church, that he gives so little evidence of his presence in the services of his house, that he allows his enemies such authority to damage the work of Christ, that he leaves us with such dry eyes and dull hearts in our gatherings. Real intercession is the result of these two things: the promise and the providence of God in seeming conflict. When the soul feels ground between the upper millstone of God's promise and the nether millstone of his providence, then it prays as it ought. The Psalms bear record to this fact. Take such examples as Psalm 44 or Psalm 74 or Psalm 89. In these instances what we have is the tension begotten in the believer's soul through the apparent inconsistency between what the Lord has promised to do for us and what he is at present doing for us. This tension creates in the longing heart the frequent cry, 'Lord, how long?'

It much glorifies God when his people call out to him to fulfil his promises in this way. It is for men who will pray like this that he looks. If he finds none, he is displeased and dishonoured. Could more terrible words be found anywhere in the Bible than these: 'The Lord saw it, and it displeased him that there was no judgement. And he saw that there was no man, and wondered that there was no intercessor'

(*Isa.* 59:15–16). Or again: 'and I sought for a man among them, that should make up the hedge, and stand in the gap before me for the land, that I should not destroy it: but I found none' (*Ezek.* 22:30).

What do such challenging words teach but that the Lord takes special delight in hearing the persistent supplications of those who will hold his own promises before his eyes and who will give him no rest till he makes his work a praise in the earth? (*Isa.* 62:7). Such are the effect of God's desertions upon prayerful people. Loud and fervent cries spring out of a soul which is indignant at the blasphemy done to God's Name by sin.

Faith becomes visible in the way it views the glory and honour of God. To small souls only our own personal matters are important. But to the Great Hearts of this world the supreme issue is the glory and the honour of God himself. It is this motive that marks the intercessions of a Moses or a David or a Samuel. It is this that we see in the prayers of a Paul, or a Luther, or a Calvin. They burn because of the boldness of the enemy. Their emotions are choked at the dishonour done to God when his truth and law, when his gospel and salvation are hidden behind a forest of lies. This is what makes a man or a woman a pleader with God. And let it not be forgotten that some of the noblest of all Bible pleaders with God were women. Let Hannah be called to mind, or Esther, or Anna in the New Testament. This last spent her whole life in pleading for the coming of the kingdom of God. A lifetime of intercession must go by before she sees her heart's desire: the birth of the long-promised Messiah. She specialised in this one thing: wrestling with the Almighty. Nor did she wrestle in vain. Though the promise tarried, yet in due time it came and her heart's desire was granted to her.

Oh that God would raise up among our nations men and women who would specialise in this gracious work of pleading the promises! Oh that the Lord would touch the hearts of many and give to them a vision of what might be done in these days if only his power and presence were again granted to us! Truth we have again in a wonderful measure. But the world passes by our doors as though this were some private interest of ours and had no relevance to the eternal destiny of men and nations.

The world will not pass us by in the hour when God rises up and puts the trumpet to his mouth once again. At this hour he sleeps and gives men over to their love of vanity. He suffers men to go on their way heedless of his Word and heedless of the claims of his Son upon their lives. This is not completely so, of course. But it is largely so. Society sees no need of God or of gospel. Sin feels right. Sin tastes delicious. Sin appeals to every faculty. But once let God arise from his long sleep and things will change in a moment, as they have done so often in the past. Our special times of intercession are with this one thing supremely in view, that he would appear again in glory (*Psa.* 102:16). It is for this we ought to give ourselves as far as we can to special intercession, that the Lord would end his long sleep and shout like a giant refreshed by wine (*Psa.* 78:65). With this in mind should we in these dark days cry out with peculiar earnestness, that he would lift up the fallen standard and give a banner to the church that may be displayed because of the truth (*Psa.* 60:4).

In his love to his own people God has given promises in a form wonderfully calculated to raise our faith and to lead us to expect great things from God. Such a promise is that of Isaiah: 'When the enemy shall come in like a flood, the Spirit of the Lord shall lift up a standard against him' (*Isa.* 59:19).

Are there any who are devoting themselves to such a ministry of prayer as we have here presented? Are there some who will see this as their great and noble life's work? Are there those who will become addicted to the ministering to the saints in this task of special pleading with God?

Never perhaps was the need for excellence in prayer among Christians greater than it is at this hour. We see daily that sin creeps, indeed that it marches, into the citadels of modern life while weak men give in to it on every hand. Sin and pride, defiance and disobedience to God's laws have a stranglehold on our modern world.

We owe it to this generation and to generations unborn to cry out to God against this wave of sin till he is pleased to stand up in his majesty once more and to command: 'Thus far shalt thou come but no farther, and here shall thy proud waves be stayed.'

18

Watch and Pray

Christians have to face each day often with a cold heart and a leaden spirit. In some cases there may be physical, and even medical, reasons for this. However, it cannot be doubted that this early morning deadness is closely connected to the fact that we are fallen and sinful creatures. Many believers, as a consequence of factors both physical and spiritual, find themselves each day at the bottom of the spiritual staircase (so to speak), and they have a hard task to lift their souls up into a more warm and feeling state. No doubt there are exceptions to this. But we suspect that it is the experience of many and, perhaps, of most.

Admitting as we do that this daily deadness is what we sinners deserve, we must assert strongly that we dare not allow ourselves to remain any day in this condition but must take deliberate daily action to bring our souls into a more spiritual and elevated condition if at all possible. Failure to do so will most certainly lead to inward backsliding and a loss of the power of grace within our hearts. This, in turn, if allowed to persist, will expose us to greater temptations and to greater liability to trespass on to the forbidden ground. The rule is that when the fire dies low, the wild beasts of the night draw nearer. And if it should ever happen that the fire were to go almost out they would attempt to devour and destroy us, if possible, altogether.

It is for this reason that the Bible says: 'Keep thy heart with all diligence for out of it are the issues of life' (*Prov.* 4:23). The soul needs daily to be armed and re-armed with 'the whole armour of God'. We here suggest that the soul needs to be reanimated every new day as a matter of regular and lifelong habit.

There are persons to whom this basic teaching is unwelcome and boring: 'Do we *still* need to be exhorted to keep a regular daily time of prayer and Bible reading? Have we not got beyond that elementary stage of the Christian life? In more mature Christians is there not a stronger *habit* of grace which has less need of what we used to call the "Quiet Time"?' The answer to these suggestions we believe to be, No. Our reasons for saying so are these. First, all our strength as believers is *borrowed* strength and needs to be applied for conscientiously each day. Secondly, as the habit of grace grows stronger so it is God's way with us to match our providences to our strength. Our temptations as more mature Christians are certain to be greater than when we were babes in Christ. Third, we read in Scripture that the falls of God's people were more frequently in their *maturity* than in their spiritual infancy. A moment's thought will confirm to us that this was so. We may call to mind Noah, Abraham, Moses, David, Solomon and Peter.

It is a fair assumption to make that God would not send his servants to fight with shoddy armour. But if we neglect to put on our armour each and every day that we go forth into this world, we have only ourselves to blame if we are badly wounded and almost killed.

The guilty truth is that too many Christians are neglecting their souls in secret. It may be that they are doing so because they have deluded themselves that they have reached a place of permanent and lifelong security. Or it may be so because they fancy that it was enough preparation for heaven to have spent their *early* Christian years cultivating a daily time of secret devotions and that now, later in life, such things are ridiculously juvenile. Or it may be because of the outward pressures of life. Whatever is the cause, we fear that the proverbial 'little bird', if he were to say what is happening among many Christians today, would have to tell us that hundreds and hundreds of Christians are failing to keep up any more the good old practice of holding secret devotions. We fear too that he would have to report that families are not, in too many cases, worshipping daily as families in their own homes. But these things ought not so to be. Our soul's life-blood is in these good practices.

There are more excuses for neglecting the soul than there are hairs upon our head and every effort is being made these days by the powers of darkness to persuade us that effort, exertion, toil and sweat are no part of a 'healthy modern Christianity'.

Observation and experience tell us, however, that when good habits are left off for any length of time they are very hard to recover. And since our carnal hearts are much opposed to all spiritual and secret duties it cannot be otherwise than that we shall find it a hundred times easier to give up our daily trysting times with God than to resume them once we have grown sick of them. The only safe way to keep a good duty up is to keep it up *always*. Let a day go by without secret prayer and it will become so much easier to let a prayerless week go by – and then a prayerless month . . . The fault and the folly was to drop a good habit even for a single day. But if we have dropped the good habit at all, we must at all costs drag ourselves back to it even it if is the case that we come to it kicking and screaming.

'Ah, but', says a voice in the soul, 'we ought not to pray to God with a reluctant spirit.' No, but better by far to pray reluctantly than not at all. If we cannot pray with fire, then at least we must still pray, even if the ashes on the altar of our hearts are cold. Better a duty done coldly than not at all.

In saying this we do not deny that we *ought* to pray always with the flame of the Spirit burning brightly upon the altar of our soul. But, we mean, if this is not our experience on any particular occasion we must set about prayer and Bible reading none the less. Secret duties are not only owed to the soul. They are owed to God, and they are owed not as courtesies but as duties. The omission of secret prayer and Bible reading is not only harmful to *us*. It is sin against God; and it would not be inconsistent with what we know of God from his Word if he were to chasten us for our neglect of these good habits by leaving us for a time till we had fallen into some alarming sin. The love of God does not promise to keep Christians from open sin if they are foolish enough to neglect their secret duty.

We pray, however, not only because we must, but because we may. Secret devotions, in spite of what we said earlier, are never *mere* duties but high and holy privileges. The soul that has found real communion with God in secret knows full well that nothing this side of eternity can compare with this experience. The problem is that we do not *always* have this exhilaration and, because this is so, we learn to pray with less and less expectation of it till we can, if we do not pull ourselves together, end up by merely 'saying our prayers'. By which expression we mean that we sink to a dead level of formalism and routine. If we do not at this point see the red light that signals danger, we shall, before long, become guilty of drifting into a state of soul in which we do nothing but utter 'prayerless prayers'.

If we are to pray habitually all through life and to pray as we ought we shall need to *enjoy* prayer. No one does for long what he does not enjoy. To pray without pleasure is 'to draw near with the lips while our heart is far from God' (*Matt.* 15:8). Somehow we shall require to set apart somewhere in the day, and perhaps like Daniel more than once in the day, when we kneel secretly before our Maker. This is something agreed on by all professing Christians in theory. But is it being really observed in practice?

The difficulty which we all seem to feel in our modern world – though we dare not admit it – is this: Where am I going to get the time from to pray to God for half an hour or so each day? The answer is simple. We all make time for what we *want* to do. Our problem is not shortage of time but of desire. To say that is a help because it points to our *real*, as distinct from our supposed, need. Our wicked unwillingness to spend time alone in the fellowship of God is the saddest evidence possible that we are fallen and ruined creatures who deeply need to be given a fresh willingness to make God our chief joy. Once we get to that point we have a heaven upon earth. The difficulty is to put the world out of our heart first.

There is no end to the inventiveness of the human heart when it comes to finding excuses for the neglect of secret prayer. Many a time we would rather die than pray. But we must pray and read our Bible every day till God calls us at length into his nearer presence. It is hard work because 'the flesh is weak' (*Mark* 14:38). Even the twelve apostles found this duty too hard for them, though they had uttered prophecies in plenty and worked miracles. Indeed, we might say, the working of miracles is 'easy' compared to the difficulty of disciplining our own hearts to act spiritually every day of life by habitually abasing ourselves in the sublime presence of the great God.

It is a mistake to pray too soon or too much for *outward* blessings of any kind or to rush into God's presence with our little lists of requests for this and that. We must begin with God's own being and strive to direct our thoughts to the realisation of what God is: his essence, his persons, his attributes, his power and his purposes. So our Saviour taught us to begin in prayer: 'Hallowed be thy name; thy kingdom come, thy will be done.'

We must rid ourselves of the mentality which chats and chatters to God like an equal. Rather, we put ourselves down very low before his great majesty. Begin always in this way. Look up to the invisible throne and engage all your emotions and powers to realise that God is the altogether holy One. Begin with God's immensity, purity, sacredness. Treat him as the great King he is. Never assume the attitude of near equality. The apostle John, who most often speaks of the love of God, fell down 'as dead' before the glory of the risen Christ (*Rev.* 1:17). It is the right way to begin. Those who begin low will find that God 'lifts them up' in prayer to the enjoyment of great boldness.

If we are to pray aright we must know our Bible well. Almost all that we know of God comes from the Bible. If we pray in any way, either as to the requests we make or the attitude we adopt, which is significantly different from prayers in the Bible, we have gone wrong and must correct ourselves. Common faults are to use God's name too often, to repeat ourselves thoughtlessly, to overwork well-worn phraseology till it loses almost all meaning. In public prayer too, it is a mistake to pray for too much or to go on too long. Only one in a hundred can pray long to the delight of those who hear him. In secret we have no human audience. But we need to watch that we do not develop bad habits in prayer even when we are alone with God on our knees.

It is a great delusion to suppose that there is no need for stated daily times of prayer in secret because we may 'pray without ceasing' (*1 Thess.* 5:17). We are to pray at regular times as a matter of spiritual duty. But, mercifully, we may then sally forth to other duties with a prayerful disposition and with many occasional prayers shot up to heaven in the course of our worldly tasks. Such, we believe, is the meaning of 'praying without ceasing'; not that we discard all set times but that we do not altogether stop praying when we have left the closet.

The Christian cannot alter many of the evils which grieve his spirit in our modern world. He cannot, though he dearly wishes to, reverse much modern legislation, to attend to matters of law and order, to rescue the unborn child, to protect women and children who are exposed to violence, to bring the wheel of discipline over the necks of evil-workers. These things he would do if he could. But he has not power to do so.

However, the Christian can and must take great pains to watch over his own soul in this sensual and slippery age when good men are finding it hard to keep to the path. There is no new or golden formula of safety. There is none promised and none needed, but only this: 'Watch and pray.' It is such elementary, familiar advice that it is easily scorned and ignored in favour of more exhilarating modern experiences of an exotic kind.

All who are going to get safely to heaven, however, know by spiritual instinct that, hard as it is to keep at, private prayer each day is essential.

THE CHRISTIAN'S ENJOYMENT OF
GRACE AND GLORY

19

Christ's Many-Sided Love

The love of Christ for his people is as mysterious and wonderful as his divine person. The Christian can no more understand how great is Christ's love for him than he can understand what it means that Christ is the eternal Son of God. Scientific experts may be able to weigh the earth or measure the oceans but there is no measuring rod for infinity, and the measurement of a Saviour's affection and attachment to those for whom he died is infinite in its scale.

It is a thousand pities that we do not stop often enough to ponder this love which our Lord and Master has for us. It would transform our present life into something more akin to heaven-on-earth if we did. We misguidedly allow our moods and feelings to be dictated by our circumstances, our health and our critics. The way to get back the lost romance of our Christian faith is to *fill* our minds with the certainty that Jesus Christ is more attached to the weakest Christian in his affections than he is to all other created beings whatsoever.

The reasons for our human affection are not always easy to give. We love for rational reasons but we cannot say what all the factors are which draw forth our affection. Natural relationship provides the first basis for our experience of love. Our hearts instinctively flow out in attachment to our mothers and fathers, our brothers and sisters. As we mature we discover our affections drawn to one outside our family circle to whom we become bound in a blessed lifelong relationship of husband or wife.

This is as high as natural love can rise. It is a great and wonderful degree of love. But it is not the highest degree of love which we can know. Religious conversion carries our affections to a higher level still. If it does not, we are not Christians because 'he who loves father or mother more than me is not worthy of me' (*Matt.* 10:37). The grace of conversion lifts our affections to a point above all natural affection. The Christian loves Christ above every other object of love.

However, the Christian's love for Christ, even at its best and at its height, is poor by comparison with His love for each one of His people. There are dimensions to Christ's love which beggar our powers of thought or imagination and yet which we do well to recall frequently. The Spirit of God speaking in the Scripture informs us of it as love in all its 'breadth, and length, and depth, and height' (*Eph.* 3:18). It is a delightful way of telling us that in whichever direction we travel we are still embraced by Christ's love and care. Though we should mount to the stars or dig deep as the deepest mines we are as Christians the objects of Christ's perfect protection and redemptive grace. The universe is too small for us as Christians to get beyond Christ's love.

The believer would do well to roll himself in this love of Jesus and wrap himself in it each day. By this we mean that he should take time daily to get his mind and heart worked up to a sense of the truth and reality of Christ's love for *him* personally. We are terribly guilty of emptying the Bible's words of their meaning and power. We end up with a mind full of great biblical terms and phrases but do not somehow savour the truth and reality of these phrases in our souls. This is true even of the oft-repeated biblical expression 'the love of Christ'. How many times we read it in God's Word – and how many times it leaves us unmoved by its sublime significance!

There is not the least excuse for our habitual coolness when in the Bible we read of Christ's love for us. It is a love which has been exhibited and displayed upon the cross. There *is* such a thing as secret love, or affection which one person has for another and yet which he never tells and never speaks about, or else never demonstrates. But Christ's affection for believers is not of this kind. While the shadow of the cross was falling upon our Saviour's spirit he pointed out to his disciples in the Upper Room that he was about to demonstrate his love to them in the highest possible way: 'Greater love hath no man than this, that a man lay down his life for his friends' (*John* 15:13). We have a Saviour whose affection for us is no mere theory. His claims are supported by compelling evidence: blood, sweat, tears and death.

We do a disservice to our Master and to our own souls when we doubt his love towards us. There are many ways of doubting his love. Sometimes we fall into the habit of regarding Christ's love as all in the past: 'He died on the cross for me a long time ago.' But the same Saviour lives today and forever with the same love for the same persons. If he loved us before we were born and died for us while as yet we were only names of lost sinners in his Book, how much more does he love us today, now that we are brought into being and into a state of grace! Does not Paul say much the same:

'For if, when we were enemies, we were reconciled to God by the death of his Son, much more, being reconciled, we shall be saved by his life' (*Rom.* 5:10)? We must not make a crucifix of Christ. His goodness towards us is not petrified in the past but is as fresh and full as when the blood streamed down his blessed face while he made good the words he had before spoken: 'For their sakes I sanctify myself . . . I lay down my life for the sheep' (*John* 17:19; 10:15).

A common fault with us is that we try to read the measure of the love of Jesus from the outward circumstances of our lives. When the sun shines we believe his love. But when the clouds gather we doubt it. When we do not see our prayers at once answered we sink into gloom and morbidity. When troubles gather all round us in a dark cluster we conclude that he has forgotten us.

It seldom occurs to us that Christ is best known when we are in trouble, pain or reproach. We forget who it was that led Israel out of Egypt through the Red Sea; or who guided them through the wilderness to the Promised Land; or who appeared with Shadrach, Meshach and Abednego in the fiery furnace; or who said to Paul in the shipwreck, 'Fear not, Paul; thou must be brought before Caesar' (*Acts* 27:24). We need to go again to Samuel Rutherford's *Letters* to call to mind that it is in the place of suffering that Jesus Christ is to be enjoyed best. Our faith is too accustomed to being only in the shallows.

By how many forgotten or else unnoticed ways does Jesus Christ prove to us his everlasting love! Have we forgotten that it was impossible for us ever to have come to him without his own power and grace? Our first signs of conviction made him rejoice. His affection towards us kindled as he saw us first learning to recognise the world's emptiness and heard our first prayers tell him that we could not bear to live without him. He rejoiced in heaven as he watched our early struggles against sin, our escape from the devil's prison-house, our ignorant and tearful efforts to find him, and in him to find life and peace. It was all his love towards us.

Only as we pause, collect our senses together and look back do we see how kindly he has led us from the hour of our first conversion till now. The wolf and the hireling have caught and deceived thousands; but they have not deceived nor devoured us. The devil has clawed back into his den many false professors and hypocrites – perhaps even before our very eyes. But the love of Jesus has ensured that no one could snatch us out of his hand (*John* 10:28). It is all his unnoticed and forgotten love to us.

And what of those moments of fiery trial and temptation when our feet almost slipped away and our will to obey wavered? The memory of some of our struggles may well bring beads of sweat out on our brow. The true believer knows that Bunyan was right when he wrote of Apollyon and the 'foul fiend', of Giant Despair and of Doubting Castle. We have all been close enough to the pilgrims in their progress towards the Celestial City to know that we too have only escaped by the skin of our teeth. It came to pass only through the love of Christ that would not suffer us to be tempted above that we were able to bear (*1 Cor.* 10:13). How little we have thanked him for it!

It is the way of men to parade their affections; but it is the 'glory of God to conceal a thing' (*Prov.* 25:2). So we discover that the Lord Jesus Christ has greater love for his people than they either know or experience in this life. Infinite love cannot be exaggerated; but it can be, and by us in this life always is, underestimated. Like children, we mistake a frown for an alteration in the affections of one we thought loved us before. But the frowns of Christ's brow are all to teach us obedience, humility and greater dependence on his grace.

It was wisely said by an old writer that Christ 'feeds us with hunger and comforts us with desertions'. This mystery is explained like this. Christ withdraws his felt presence only to bid us run after him faster. He starves us of felt comforts so that we may be satisfied with no comforts but his own presence.

The danger which we face is that we want peace and joy rather too much. We are not mature in our knowledge of Christ till we have come to see that it is possible to make an idol of our peace. The immature, inexperienced Christian wants peace (which is right and good). But he wants it at too high a price if he seeks it where it ought not to be found.

It is possible for a Christian to seek, and for a while, to enjoy peace and joy without Christ. So Paul warns the Corinthians: 'Now ye are full, now ye are rich, ye have reigned as kings without us: and I would to God ye did reign, that we also might reign with you' (*1 Cor.* 4:8). They were 'happy' and 'triumphant' but there was more of the flesh in it than of the genuine love of Christ. How different the experiences of the apostles: 'We are fools for Christ's sake . . . we are weak . . . we are despised' (*1 Cor.* 4:10)! There is sometimes more of Christ's love in our hard circumstances than in our elated feelings. The proof will be seen in our deeper attachment, or otherwise, to his person, his truth and his cause.

The worst way to judge of Christ's love in this life is to go by outward things therefore. Surely Solomon taught us this in these words: 'No man knoweth either love or hatred by all that is before them. All things come alike to all: there is one event to the righteous, and to the wicked; to the good and to the clean, and to the unclean; to him that sacrificeth, and to him that sacrificeth not: as is the good, so is the sinner; and he that sweareth, as he that feareth an oath' (*Eccles.* 9:1b, 2). The Christian who expects Christ to make him richer than others, or healthier than others, or freer from troubles than others is ignorant of the first principles of Christ's love.

The fact is that no one knows whom Christ loves or hates by the outward circumstances of life. The evidence of Christ's love is that we have our wills subdued to obedience, that we be made sound in faith and sincere in our service. It may be that the Lord will take stern measures to produce this godly character in us at times. It may also be that those who today enjoy a full cup of religious mirth will not be most full of Christ's love in the end. Here, as in similar things, 'the first shall be last and the last first' (*Matt.* 19:30).

The state of grace is a mysterious condition in which things are not as they seem and are not as we commonly feel them to be. The reason is that in the state of grace we are being taught to 'walk by faith, not by sight' (*2 Cor.* 5:7).

But the state of glory will be far different. There the infinite love of Christ to each particular believer will be full to capacity. Every pot – the great and the small – will be full to the very brim. All that we long to feel of a Saviour's love will be felt forever more and more to all eternity. Add to this that then we too shall love the great Jesus with a perfect love which knows no cooling moods and which will experience neither clouds nor fluctuation.

As heaven is a growing state so it must be a state in which the many-sided love of Christ is to be known by the saints more and more fully forever. We have one foot in heaven now. Let us see that we get wholly there.

20

Feeling Christ's Love Afresh

No experience of a Christian is more profitable to the soul than to feel afresh Christ's love for him. Yet no experience is so neglected in our day. The reason for this is because of our pride and ignorance of Christ as a living Saviour. As a generation of believers we resemble the disciples of Christ before his resurrection rather than after it. This must be a sign that something is wrong with our understanding of the truth which we profess. We take our Christianity more from one another than from the Bible. We live on the shadowy side of Christian experience rather than in the full light of what is possible to attain to. What would Samuel Rutherford make of us? What would M'Cheyne or Spurgeon, both so full of Christ's love, have to say of us? It is time that we took ourselves in hand.

The reasons why we are dead to a sense of Christ's love, we have said above, is because of our pride and our ignorance of Christ himself. Surely we must admit that this is so. There is in us, even after conversion, a sinful reluctance to take the time and trouble necessary to have our hearts brought into a *feeling* state. We learn to be content with *head knowledge* of Christian truth, and we allow ourselves to be bullied by the unfeeling Christianity all round us into thinking that *emotions* accompanying faith must be a mark of excess. For some reason we who live in the modern world are afraid of emotion. We suppose it to be a virtue to stifle tears of conviction, to suppress all talk about Christ's visits to the soul, to make it a crime to express excitement when we receive tokens of God's love to us.

It is possible to be sound in our profession of the truth yet immature in our emotional response to it. When this is true of any Christian it is a sign that he or she has not yet understood how the truth of God ought to affect us.

It was a good saying of the English martyr, John Bradford, that he made it his rule not to go away from any duty before he had *felt* something of Christ in it. He meant, of course, that he strove, when he prayed, always to have his heart aflame before he left off praying and that he would not lay his Bible or book down before he had felt his heart burning within him (*Luke* 24:32). Spurgeon informs us in one of his sermons on the Song of Solomon that the famous Bernard of Clairvaux used to say to Christ: 'I never go away from thee without thee.' By these quaint words he meant that he waited on Christ till he had a lively sense of Him, which followed him after his devotions were over. Such expressions as the above take us to the heart of our subject.

The above-quoted sayings of Bradford and Bernard assume something which is not always very readily assumed by modern Christians, that it is possible and very desirable to get our hearts worked up with holy emotion in this way. Christ is not a mere doctrine, it must be remembered. He is a risen, glorified Saviour. His love for us today is as great and as real as at the time when he was suffering for us on the cross. He is as much 'with us' and ministering to us by his Spirit as in the days of his flesh.

We would all regard the Gospels as very much the poorer if they were purged of all the rich human emotion which they portray. Suppose Jesus had never wept over Jerusalem or at the grave of Lazarus. Suppose Mary of Bethany had not devoutly poured out her ointment over the Saviour's body, or that Mary Magdalene had not felt enough of Christ's love to be early at the tomb weeping for his 'absence'. Imagine if the penitent woman of Luke 7 had not come into Simon's house to wash our Lord's feet with her tears and wipe them with her long, beautiful hair. Would these four wonderful Gospels not be greatly weakened in the power and fascination which they exert over us? If the Lord of glory had not been shown to us as sweating and groaning in the course of his mighty wrestlings to deal with our sin and liability to eternal death, would we not be vastly poorer in our understanding of his love for us? Emotion is not suppressed in the Bible and we have no right to ignore its place in the lives of Bible characters – or our own.

The things of God are all great and mighty things, and they should exert a great and mighty influence upon us in every way. The Bible is not a quarry for scholars to research in and nothing more. It is not a textbook for religious education only. It is not simply a fountain of proof-texts. It is a God-given account of how he himself has taken steps to redeem us from death and hell, to translate us from darkness unto light, to lift us from sin to grace and from grace to glory at last. All of this stupendous divine plan is concentrated on the person of the Lord Jesus Christ, our beloved Saviour. He is its Alpha and its Omega. He is its Yea and its Amen. Surely we cannot, dare not, must not allow ourselves to read the Bible, which speaks of him, and not also make it our regular rule and practice to *feel* some of his love to us as we read it.

One of the reasons why men read the Bible and feel nothing as they read it is that they do not approach it in the right way and with the right understanding. We should see Christ in the Bible everywhere. He is present at the beginning of time as our Creator. He is the One worshipped by the patriarchs. Abraham, like all before and after him in Old Testament times, 'rejoiced to see Christ's day' (*John* 8:56). They had an understanding of God's plan and in it they saw Christ as their coming Saviour and Messiah. The Mosaic rituals all speak to us of Christ. Every drop of sacrificial blood shed in olden times was emblematic of Christ's blood. All the offices of theocratic man – kings, priests, prophets – shadowed forth aspects of the Saviour's person and work. All prophecies and oracles were preparatory in one way or another to the coming of Jesus Christ to perform his magnificent ministry of redemption. To read the Bible with academic, critical or other interests to the forefront of our minds is to miss the mark and to lose the blessing. We are above all to read the Bible so as to 'meet' Christ in it. It is because we are too often 'fools and slow of heart to believe' that the Scriptures all point to Jesus that we put them down without our hearts having been stirred within us.

Shame on us as a generation of professing Christians if we can get excited more about other things than about the love of Christ! But it is often the case that professing Christians *are*. The lust of many other things enters in and love for Christ grows cold. Minutes are spent on prayer; hours on sport. Minutes are left for Bible reading and (if at all) for family worship; hours are given over to watching television. It is time to take stock and to throw out the challenge: When will we begin to climb higher? Who among us will break the mould of Christian mediocrity and reach for the high examples set for us by our great Reformed forefathers?

It is possible to enjoy much more of Christ's love and to be much more full of his Holy Spirit than most are at this hour. There is not a church in the country or in the world that does not need to see more shining faces than they see at present. The greatest need we all have is for more of the burning heart. It cannot be concealed when it exists. It will show itself in unctuous prayers, in heavenly talk, in holy living, in fervent affection, in patient suffering and in ardent hoping for blessing from God. There is today great talk about 'love', but small experience of it. Yet it is only as we ourselves burn with a felt sense of Christ's love to us that we shall radiate that love to others. Steel is molten in the furnace and so must the soul become incandescent in the fire of Christ's love before it can burn as it needs to do.

There is a terrible reluctance to talk seriously about godly emotion in the modern church. This is very strange when we recall that excitement and enthusiasm are expected everywhere else in life. Who ever heard of audiences attending sporting events without excitement? Or popular places of entertainment? Theatres, operas, concerts, film – all attract crowds because they generate emotion in the human heart for a few brief hours. And shall we who know Christ as our glorified Lord and God be the only people on earth to suppress our feelings in a flat monotony of emotional dullness?

It was not so in the great ages of the church that are past. The early church had experience of Christ's presence in a felt manner. They knew of 'love shed abroad in the heart' (*Rom.* 5:5), 'peace that passeth all understanding' (*Phil.* 4:7), 'joy unspeakable and full of glory' (*1 Pet.* 1:8), 'boldness' such as men have only after being much in the presence of Christ

(*Acts* 4:13). The first Christians were like men 'full of new wine' (*Acts* 2:13). They dealt a death blow to men's consciences by the power of their testimony and 'turned the world upside down' by their proclamation of the gospel (*Acts* 17:6). That they did so, that the Reformers later did so and that the Methodists after them did so can only be explained by one thing: they were men who *felt* the love of Christ and were constrained by it. Such things may well put us to shame in our day.

It will not do to excuse our low levels of spiritual emotion to say that some groups of Christians let their emotions dictate to them or that they run to extremes. Let our heads be filled with knowledge and our memories with instruction. Let our bookshelves be laden with all the best books and our hours spent in reading them. But let all this include a belief in the place of spiritual affections in a believer's life. Truth may, and must, be studied so as to set our souls *on fire*. There is nothing at all in the Christian's life more important than the enjoyment of Christ's love. If our reading and our studying do not lead us many a time into 'wonder, love and praise', we lack understanding and are coming short.

Of the many aids available to us to correct an unfeeling state of soul, we may mention two: meditation and godly conversation. The one we may do on our own privately, the other in the company of other Christians. By meditation, we refer to the practice of concentrating our thoughts on one or other of the great doctrines of the gospel till our hearts are affected. This is not emotionalism or contrived spirituality. It is to gather honey from the comb. A little time spent in this way, either at home or as we work, may lift our spirits to heaven. 'As I mused the fire burned' (*Psa.* 39:3). Our great Puritan divines did much in this way. In our busy age we dare not neglect it.

When in Christian company we should make it our general rule to raise the conversational level to spiritual subjects, especially to subjects which are best fitted to warm the affection. Having got into a spiritual theme of conversation be sure to keep it there. Do not lower the tone of conversation to ordinary subjects. As we practise this habit of spiritual conversation we shall find our aptitude and our appetite both increasing in it. It is the pattern which our Saviour himself gives us in the Gospels. He never utters 'an idle word'. Everything that drops from his lips is good for edifying. It is a very high standard to aim at but we must practise it for ourselves one with another as Christians.

As we do these things we shall find many a time that 'Jesus himself draws near' by his Spirit. Is it not what he himself promised: 'Then they that feared the Lord spake often one to another: and the Lord hearkened, and heard it, and a book of remembrance was written before him for them that feared the Lord, and that thought upon his name' (*Mal.* 3:16)? Ryle somewhere speaks critically of some Christians who 'in conference add nothing' (*Gal.* 2:6). It is a poor testimonial to have if we do not edify one another by affectionate spiritual talk when we meet one another as believers.

There will always be some who despise the things that we have been discussing here. But they are not our examples to follow. Rather let us expect that from time to time as we wait on the Lord we shall find him wonderfully close to us to give us fresh draughts of his love and to rise upon us 'with healing in his wings' (*Mal.* 4:2).

Would that he might visit us all more often and put the cup of spiritual expression to our lips. His love is 'better than wine' (*Song of Sol.* 1:2).

21

The Taste of Grace

A Christian is a person who is surprised at himself and who can never fully understand himself. This is true at the time of his conversion, when he becomes aware of the overshadowing hand of God upon his life leading him from sin to Christ. The believer's experience is of being called into an unexpected path of life. At first it may be very unwelcome to him. He will probably fight against the call of God, resenting it as an interference and an interruption in his own plans and ambitions. But at length his vain struggles end in calm resignation. He becomes willing to be led he knows not where or how. He surrenders his life to Jesus Christ and acquiesces in the unseen and conquering will of God which has now finally mastered him.

Most believers can never forget the time and place of their first awakening by God. As Jacob always remembered his experience at Bethel and as Paul could not stop marvelling at the heavenly vision of Christ on the Damascus road, so the child of God often goes back in his own mind to the occasion of his first coming to know the Lord. It is his secret, shared with those of like precious faith and sometimes with the ignorant whom he wishes to be similarly blessed. But there are instincts within him which lead him to feel that such pearls of sacred experience must not be cast before those who would trample on them like swine.

One of the earlier discoveries made by the child of God after his conversion is that he has entered a world of new and sanctified emotions. The things which were to him in the past so dry and unrewarding have now taken on a new dimension of life and freshness. Secret prayer, fellowship with his fellow believers, attending to Bible reading and the preaching of the Word of God are now all things which bring a *felt* blessing to his soul. Previously it was not so – or, at least, not so in the way and in the measure it is now. Before conversion he went to prayer as a boy goes to school, with a heavy heart and dragging his feet to it. Preaching was in those days a sort of purgatory to be endured for the sake of appearances. But he had no heart for it and no felt good out of it. The real truth was that he secretly yearned for the day when he could leave home and become conveniently 'too busy' to attend church regularly. But conversion changes that by making all spiritual things enjoyable and desirable.

The truth is that the newly converted man has started to experience the taste of grace communicated to him now for the first time. The means of grace (the Word, sacraments, fellowship and prayer), which were once lifeless and drab to him are now found to contain a sweetness like milk and honey. They do not merely feed him but cheer him. Though still on occasion the child of God may read and pray without feeling, he knows from past experience that feelings are to be had in these means of grace. He recalls those times when he bent his knees before the Father of spirits and found a rush of the Spirit into his soul which astonished and excited him as much as if he had seen an angel or stood for a few moments beside the sea of glass. He has amongst his treasured memories some moments when he read the Bible with so much help and profit that it stopped his breath. Time stood still, earth shrank beneath his feet, heaven was about him and he knew that the eternal world was close at hand.

The taste of grace comes as something of a surprise at first. We had previously thought, as men without Christ, that pleasure was only to be had in the world. But to our astonishment after our conversion we become conscious of a new and better pleasure, an excitement which does not cloy or leave a bitter taste in the mouth. It is a tasting that the Lord is gracious (*Psa.* 34:8) and that Jesus our Saviour is all sweetness (*1 Pet.* 2:7). The life of the believer (so we come to find after our conversion) is like the ancient Tabernacle, unimpressive from the outside but full of life, light and divine mystery when we are within. And the experience of the new convert is to realise that he *is* now within, in the place where shed blood atones for sin, where there is a laver which continues to cleanse our guilt, when prayer ascends to God's ear acceptably, where he eats the bread of fellowship with the Lord and where he can draw near with holy boldness into the sacred presence of Jehovah.

If at first the young Christian is content to feel the consoling love of God upon his heart when he draws near in worship and if, because he is still only a babe, he thinks more about his new enjoyment of soul than of the God who gives them to him, he will learn a better way as he matures. When still young we are apt to idolise 'the peace which passes all understanding' (*Phil.* 4:7) and the 'joy unspeakable and full of glory' (*1 Pet.* 1:8). All our life as Christians we shall have a relish for the experience of God's love 'shed abroad in our heart' (*Rom.* 5:5) and for a sense of 'the powers of the world to come' (*Heb.* 6:5). It is not surprising that it should be so for we are the children of God and are born to these things from above. But in our early days we are inclined to enjoy our enjoyments too much.

But the passing of time teaches the believer there is something higher than these things. It is to set our affections wholly on God himself. The distinction is not artificial. All the great Christian writers speak of it. We dare not trust our 'frames' or our feelings. We dare not 'rest' in them in case we idolise them. We must make an idol of nothing, but direct all our affections towards God alone.

It is the proof that we have matured a little when we have passed from love of comfort to contentment with the will of God. To say the same thing another way, it is proof of advancing grace when we consciously prefer the path of pure obedience to all other things. This is perhaps not an easy transition for the maturing Christian to make. When we are spiritual children the Lord may well feed us with the honey of comfort and warmth in a measure which we may have to go without at some times later on. There are other lessons to be learnt besides those of comfort. We need to become acquainted with the deceitfulness of our own hearts, the strength of indwelling sin, the suddenness of temptation and the sharpness of the world's dislike of us.

As the eagle stirs up her nest at the right time and prepares her nestlings for the experience of flight, so the Lord knows the right time to rouse his people for usefulness, service and privilege (*Deut.* 32:11). How painful did we find it to have to leave the nest of nursery protection! How surprised we were when the Lord began to stir up the nest and thrust us out to exercise our feeble wings in the first sorties of more mature understanding, suffering and faith! It seemed at the time that we were stripped of all our previous comforts, enjoyments, emotions and excitements.

Only gradually did the realisation dawn on us that we had before made too much of our experiences of delight. Then also we discovered that God had not withdrawn these earlier joys altogether. He was teaching us rather to trust him in the dark day and in the time of trouble as well as when our emotions overflowed with consolation. Slowly and painfully did we come to see that we had been before ignorant of the deeper counsels of God's Word, immature in our prayers, self-interested in our wish for a 'happy' frame of mind always and inexperienced in putting on the whole armour of God.

Faith sickens and grows pale when we refuse to follow the leading of God into the more mature experiences of his grace. One meets older Christians who are still clinging to their nursery experiences. Their prayers, their judgements, their capacity for service all reflect the fact that they never could bear to part with their immaturities. For them the words of the apostle, 'Let us go on unto perfection' were never given a place in their *hearts* (*Heb.* 6:1). What gave them intense delight at the infant stage of their Christian life is resorted to still: the babyish chorus, the elementary sermon, the 'happy' fellowship, the entertaining novelty. But the sight of older Christians still gathering at the nursery door is disappointing and disturbing. There is a time for being in the nursery, but that time is not all our life.

The appetite for grace matures in this way: we make less of the creature and more of God himself. The grown Christian lives out all his days as in the presence of the ever-blessed Triune God. His mind dwells constantly on the excellence of these three sacred Persons of Father, Son and Holy Spirit. He loves to go backward in time to the sovereign plan drawn up before all ages in which he was chosen in Christ by God. He delights to think forward to the coming world of glory when he shall be in the presence of this gracious, electing God.

The thought of the Father's love, of the Saviour's grace, of the Spirit's fellowship are now the unfailing supply of his deepest delight and confidence. Emotions he has in plenty but he has now learnt to love God more than emotions. He will live, serve, suffer and, if needs be, die to please and honour his Maker. If God gives him a taste of heaven along the path of duty, he takes it thankfully. If God denies him this feeling of elation for a while, he takes it patiently. To have God himself, so he now knows, is better than to have gracious experiences.

The time is short after all. He who rides to be crowned does not mind a few rainy hours along the route. We are soon to 'see the King in his beauty' and to 'behold the land that is very far off' (*Isa.* 33:17). The taste of grace is good. The taste of glory will be better still. Nothing about us here is perfect. Repentance is still the fitting garment for us to wear until the very end. Let us rest in nothing we have done, or read, or experienced, or felt, or known so far. Forgetting the past enjoyments even of grace, let us 'press toward the mark' (*Phil.* 3:14), bending every nerve to do the will of God while still we may. A trumpet of jubilee is soon to sound. Then may the gospel worker relax for ever and enter into the eternal enjoyment of God in Christ.

22

Christians Will Never Be Orphans

O ur Lord and Saviour Jesus Christ is still acting for us as a priest. We tend to think that Jesus finished his priestly work after he had died for us on the cross; and we then allow ourselves to suppose that he is now reigning, not as a priest, but as a king. The correct way to look at Christ's work is to see that he is a king and also a priest both before and after his sufferings on the cross.

One of the New Testament passages which make clear the ongoing priesthood of our Saviour is Hebrews 8:1–2: 'Now of the things which we have spoken this is the sum: We have such an high priest, who is set on the right hand of the throne of the Majesty in the heavens; A minister of the sanctuary, and of the true tabernacle, which the Lord pitched, and not man.' The apostle here sets forth Christ as our great high priest, acting for us in the mysterious heavenly sanctuary above. The thought is not that he has completed his priestly ministry but that he is still engaged in it for us: 'We have *such* an high priest, who is set on the right hand of the throne . . .' (v. 1).

The word 'such' here calls attention to all that the writer has been saying concerning Christ in this Epistle. He alludes to the sublime and glorious character of a priest who is both

God and man, who is infinite in worth as the eternal Son of God and yet who is perfect in his tenderness and sympathy for his beloved people because he himself is 'all of one' (*Heb.* 2:11) with us. It is such a priest, he argues, that we now 'have', not 'had'. Jesus, our priest, '*now* appears in the presence of God for us' (*Heb.* 9:24). It is a priesthood which is still active and still necessary.

The reference to the Old Testament tabernacle is instructive. The apostle must mean that there is a correspondence between the old tabernacle and that place where Christ now ministers in heaven. He can speak of this as 'the true tabernacle' (*Heb.* 8:2). By 'true' here he does not mean that the tabernacle of Moses' day was false, as though not given by divine revelation. On the contrary, Moses, he states, had to make the tabernacle 'according to the pattern showed to him in the mount' (*Heb.* 8:5). God long ago in Moses' day prescribed a 'pattern', or blueprint, to which the old tabernacle must strictly conform.

The reason for all this, states the apostle, is because the old tabernacle had to 'serve unto the example and shadow of heavenly things' (*Heb.* 8:5). So the heavenly sanctuary is described as 'the *true* tabernacle' (v. 2). It is the great spiritual reality of which the earthly tabernacle was but a type and shadow. And Christ is the great high priest now engaged in an ongoing priestly ministry of which all the priestly ministries of old were the types and shadows. So much appears clearly to be the apostle's meaning and it points to the fact that the Lord Jesus is active for us still as our priest in the heavenly sanctuary of glory.

The tabernacle itself, by its very construction, gives us a clue as to the nature of Christ's continuing priestly activity. It had two altars, one of brass and one of gold. On the brass altar were offered up the sacrificial victims – bulls and goats and sheep, duly slaughtered, cut into their pieces and placed on the fire. These slaughtered and burnt victims were the symbols of Christ's glorious atonement and death for our sins upon the cross.

Upon the second, or golden, altar was burnt incense. Hence it was termed 'the incense altar' (*Exod.* 37:25).

The incense represented the prayers of the people of God and the fragrant smoke of the burning incense rising up symbolised the ascent of the prayers before God in heaven and their acceptance before him as sweet and fragrant. However feeble our prayers seem to men, they are acceptable to God when they are offered up in reliance upon the sacrificial death of the Lord Jesus Christ. This is the lesson which Israel of old was taught by the altar of incense, and the believer today needs the same reassurance: 'Let my prayer be set forth before thee as incense' (*Psa.* 141:2).

No doubt we are right, too, to say that the golden altar represented the intercession of Christ for us in his priestly ministry. The prayers of Christ and of his people are, after all, prayers for the same things and to the same God. The merits are all Christ's. But the incense of genuine prayer ascends continually from the church on earth and it mingles with and unites with the priestly ministry of our glorified Redeemer as he intercedes for us above. It is joint prayer, both Christ's and the church's, that God's kingdom will come and his name will be glorified.

In the priestly ritual prescribed for the annual Day of Atonement there was a requirement that the fire of the brazen altar and the incense be brought closely together: 'He [the high priest] shall take a censer full of burning coals of fire from off the altar before the Lord, and his hands full of sweet incense beaten small, and bring it within the vail: And he shall put the incense upon the fire before the Lord, that the cloud of the incense may cover the mercy seat that is upon the testimony, that he die not: And he shall take of the blood of the bullock, and sprinkle it with his finger upon the mercy seat eastward; and before the mercy seat shall he sprinkle of the blood with his finger seven times' (*Lev.* 16:12–14). The finished sacrifice offered up on the brazen altar formed the basis upon which the high priest approached the presence of God to appear for the people. The incense and the blood were both necessary elements in the ceremony for removing the people's sin and giving them acceptance and favour with God.

Here is the light which we need to understand the nature of Christ's continuing priesthood in 'the true sanctuary'. On earth he died for us. He uttered the triumphant cry, 'It is finished!' The atonement which he made was then complete and perfect. To it nothing needs now to be added. But, in the glory above, our Saviour in his priestly office 'appears in the presence of God for us' (*Heb.* 9:24). This presence before God guarantees that all for whom he died are blessed with the fruits of his passion and come to grace and glory. In his ongoing priestly ministry Christ intercedes that all those whom the Father has given him should have the benefits of his once-for-all death applied to them.

The present priestly ministry then of our Saviour is one of pleading our cause on high. For that reason he is referred to in the New Testament as an 'advocate with the Father' (*1 John* 2:1). While we are on earth we are still sinful. This sin is offensive to God and to our own consciences. How are we to cope when we have such a continual volume of sin in our lives? The answer is that we must resort to the God-given advocacy of our Saviour in the glory. His obedience and blood are the basis of his pleadings with the Father that our many and grievous sins should be fully pardoned.

This is the divine and perfect remedy, and it has in it these two aspects: Christ, as priest, has atoned for our sins; and he now acts day by day as our advocate, urging that his blood be acceptable with God for our full pardon. We shall need this Christ to be a priest for us till the day when we shall be incapable of sinning any more. Till that blessed hour arrives we must rest daily and hourly on his priestly activity on high.

So weak are we as Christians in this dangerous world that we require to have, not just one advocate, but two. Our Saviour referred to this provision in his Upper Room discourse before he returned to the Father: 'And I will pray the Father, and he shall give you another Comforter, that he may abide with you for ever; Even the Spirit of truth; whom the world cannot receive, because it seeth him not, neither knoweth him: but ye know him; for he dwelleth with you, and shall be in you' (*John* 14:16–17). The word here translated 'Comforter' is the same as that translated 'advocate' in 1 John 2:1 (*parakletos*). The reason for the provision of this second Advocate is the weak condition in which we should be if he were not sent to us here on earth: 'I will not leave you *comfortless*' (*John* 14:18). The word is 'orphans', those who are proverbially defenceless and feeble. So a second Advocate is given to us by our priestly Lord in order to stand up for us and speak up for us in this life. For such is the work of one who is a 'paraclete' (literally, 'one called to the assistance of another').

The nature of the Holy Spirit's work as our advocate is explained by our Lord in the same Upper Room discourse: 'And when he is come, he will reprove the world of sin, and of righteousness, and of judgment: Of sin, because they believe not on me; Of righteousness, because I go to my Father, and ye see me no more; Of judgment, because the prince of this world is judged' (*John* 16:8–11). The Spirit will make the witness and preaching of God's people a forceful influence in the world. However weak we feel our influence as Christians to be, the Second Advocate will ensure that that influence will be felt in men's hearts and consciences. There is a secret agency behind our testimony to the gospel which guarantees that our words carry weight with the unbelieving world. We are not undefended orphans in a hostile world. Our witness to the truths of God's Word are being accompanied and sustained in this world by an all-powerful advocate, the Spirit of God himself.

The advocacy of the Spirit is subjective. It is an advocacy in men's hearts, confirming to them the truths of Scripture which the people of God preach and bear witness to. Perhaps also we should add that this advocacy works in our own experience as Christians in that, when we are attacked for our faith, the Spirit brings to mind texts of Scripture which 'comfort' and help us. Often in this way we are enabled to speak to our adversaries more wisely than we know and are given the ability to defend ourselves as God's people with skill and success. Accordingly, our Lord says: 'I will give you a mouth and wisdom, which all your adversaries shall not be able to gainsay [contradict] nor resist' (*Luke* 21:15).

The advocacy of the Spirit is subjective too in the way by which he prompts us as Christians to pray. Hence the apostle writes: 'Likewise the Spirit also helpeth our infirmities: for we know not what we should pray for as we ought: but the Spirit itself maketh intercession for us with groanings which cannot be uttered' (*Rom.* 8:26). The Spirit acts as Second

Advocate here in 'helping our infirmities'. He 'makes intercession for us', not by offering prayer *for* us but by inspiring prayer *in* us. It is we who offer the prayer, but the Spirit who creates *in* us the yearning to pray. He does this by filling the soul with inexpressible groanings to God for help and blessing. These groanings may be too hard for us to put into words. But they are the language of the regenerate heart and they are completely intelligible to God (*Rom.* 8:27). Our best prayers may well be those which we hardly find words to express properly but which are full of our sincerest groanings and longings.

Christ's advocacy, on the other hand, is objective. It is outside of us and is carried on by him as he exercises his priestly work for us within the veil. This priestly advocacy he will not cease from for an instant while the church is incomplete on earth.

However evil the world may grow, the people of God are well provided for. Against all enemies we have the prevailing ministry of two heavenly advocates. We shall never be orphans.

23

Our State of Probation

This present world is a place of probation. Here all men are on trial. So long as we remain in this world we are on mercy's ground. Once we pass beyond death there will be no alteration of our state forever. The soul that passes beyond the boundary of death is at once confirmed in its moral and spiritual condition. 'He that is unjust', will God's voice then say, 'let him be unjust still: and he which is filthy, let him be filthy still: and he that is righteous, let him be righteous still: and he that is holy, let him be holy still' (*Rev.* 22:11). Once the soul passes beyond the point of death it is confirmed in its condition eternally, either for better or for worse.

That this present life is one of trial or probation is evident from the fact that moral and spiritual changes are here going on all the time. Here in this world there are momentous changes occurring daily. Sinners are being saved. Saved sinners are being sanctified. Unsound converts are backsliding into the world. Sections of the visible church are tumbling backwards into apostasy. The bad may here, in this present world, become good before they leave it; the apparently good may, before they leave it, fall into scandalous sin and scandalous denial of the truth. Here in this life of probation all sorts of changes can be seen all round us, either for better or worse, and they illustrate the fact that our present life in this world is an unfinished state.

The unfinished condition of our present world is a source of annoyance, or at any rate of discomfort, to all who live in it. Sinners without Christ find it irksome and inconvenient to have to live alongside saints. They would prefer to have a world in which there are no saints, no churches, no Bibles and no moral restraints. It would suit them well to live in a world where the true God is not mentioned, prayer not a duty, preaching never heard, conscience never challenged. The sinner's idea of paradise is a world of pleasure without God. As far as he is able he is at work all his lifetime to bring about such a paradise. It is irritating to him to discover that Christians are actively opposing his schemes by their preaching and by their continual endeavours to promote righteousness.

Similarly, the unfinished state of this world is uncomfortable for God's people. They do their best to bear it and to be cheerful. But it is vexatious for them every day to know that their unconverted neighbours live and labour to spoil what good there is left in this world. It is frustrating for them to see that what they themselves are striving to build is being obstructed, and sometimes thrown down, by non-Christians all around them.

Such however is the nature of our life in this world of probation. The good must live here with the bad and the bad with the good. The saint and the sinner have to make the best of one another's company. There is good for them both in living side by side in this way. For the evil man it is good that he sees examples of goodness and is forced to realise that he ought to be better than he is. Were there no salt in the earth there would be little to prevent the immediate and total rot of all mankind.

It is also good for the saint to have to live for a little while in the presence of evil men. It affords him room to exercise all his graces, especially his patience. In heaven there will be no opportunity for patience to exercise itself either in God or in man. If God is able to exercise patience towards evil men in this life, much more should Christians. Though we 'vex our souls' in seeing and hearing things which are offensive to us, we must try to remember that it will not be for long. The sinner will not have long to spoil God's world. And the saint will not have long to suffer in it. 'The end of all things is at hand' (*1 Pet.* 4:7). 'The night is far spent, the day is at hand' (*Rom.* 13:12). 'The fashion of this world passeth away' (*1 Cor.* 7:31).

The purpose of God in giving us this probationary state is to prepare us for our future, eternal and unchangeable state. If there were no possibility of a moral and spiritual change in man here, there could be no gospel. For none could be converted. None could repent. None could turn to God for mercy. But God, in his boundless and wonderful grace, has given to mankind this probationary state. No such favour, let us recall, was given to the angels who sinned. They were given neither time nor opportunity for repentance, but were 'cast down to hell, and delivered . . . into chains of darkness, to be reserved unto judgement' (*2 Pet.* 2:4).

A probationary state, however uncomfortable it may feel at times to those who are passing through it, is a very wonderful and great mercy. It means, to mention but one aspect of it, that we may live in hope concerning our unconverted loved ones so long as they are alive and on mercy's ground. Here in this world it is a blessed possibility that the worst haters of Christ may yet become his most faithful servants. It happened in the case of Saul, who became Paul. It has happened to a John Newton and to a multitude of other saved sinners. It will doubtless happen a million times and more to elect persons still unborn. It is a richly comforting reason why, in our probationary state, we should be patient in adversity and cheerful in affliction. It is this comforting argument which God uses with his slain saints who cry 'How long?' from under the altar: 'It was said unto them that they should rest yet for a little season, until their fellow servants also and their brethren, that should be killed as they were, should be fulfilled' (*Rev.* 6:11).

The people of God feel the force of this argument and they derive the most solid comfort from it. No argument could weigh so much with them as this. Present trials are permitted so that our elect brothers and sisters for whom Christ, *our* Christ, died, may be brought to salvation as we are. This is an argument to blunt the sharpness of all our present afflictions. While we groan under a sense of the outrage done to God and to the godly, God is carrying the gospel to his chosen people all over the world. Missionaries live and toil under the scorching sun and under biting frosts. They fall ill, are reviled, outlawed, killed and buried. But their message lives on. Livingstone, Carey, Martyn, Brainerd . . . are all gone. But this message lives on in the hearts of millions of those whose ancestors belittled them and ill-treated them. So it will do when their modern counterparts are gone. Present agonies belong to our probationary state. Yet these agonies are offset by the gathering out of elect sinners who must share the coming glory with us.

The Bible everywhere teaches us that by faith we must look beyond this present unfinished state to the final condition in which we are all to be in a very little while. The secret of living here and now is to keep our eye firmly on what is very shortly to happen. This is the art of spiritual-mindedness. And none, let it be remembered, do so much earthly good as those who are heavenly-minded. A great part of spiritual-mindedness is to keep ever in our thoughts the prodigiously great changes which are very soon to happen to us all. When God brings down the curtain on our present probationary state, all life's actors, whether great or small, must go off the stage wearing their same costumes for ever.

The wicked will then be petrified in character and doomed to live with unmitigated wickedness, within and without and all around them to all eternity. They will have the wicked world which they wanted but they will have it in a way they do not want – full of pain and torment and with the fearful realisation that they might, while in their state of probation on earth, have found God's mercy if only they had wanted it then.

The wicked are now, in their state of probation, being 'fitted' for hell (*Rom.* 9:22). When they leave their trial period here they go, not to an alien state, but to their 'own place' (*Acts* 1:25). After this life the wicked, being unchangeably wicked, will have to live eternally without the comfortable presence of God. They go to their long home, where – alas! – they belong.

In our present condition, the above thought of an endless punishment for Christless men is a burden to us as Christians. Strange to say, those who are not going to hell are in this life more affected by the prospect of it than those who are. The wicked are blind and they are led by Satan down a winding staircase so that they do not see the bottom till they get there.

The Christian foresees the latter end of Christless men and is deeply affected by the thought of it. It is right that here in our probationary state, we should suffer at the prospect of the coming torments of the wicked. This is what constrains men to deny themselves the ordinary pleasures of life and to devote themselves to the service of the gospel. The plight of unbelievers must compel us to be serious, to be in earnest, to live like men who believe God's Word. The plight of unbelievers must constrain us to preach as dying men to dying men. The Christian, who will have no hell, now goes through mental agony because he sees hell coming upon countless of his fellow men.

Our probationary condition ends as soon as we leave this world. The believer's soul is then immediately confirmed in perfect holiness and is lifted beyond the possibility of ever sinning again. The holiness which in this life we have sought but have not perfectly attained to will then be ours at once, fully and forever. This will be a very great part, though not the whole, of our blessedness in the glory. The believer, being righteous, will be fixed by God's power in a state of immutable righteousness and, being holy, in a state of immutable holiness.

This will be the ultimate condition of every child of God. In that state we shall be beyond temptation, trial and sin. It will be a better state than that of the angels at their creation or of our first parents in Eden before the Fall. For them sin was not yet a reality but it was a possibility. For Christians who get safely beyond their present probation, sin will be only a memory and no more. Beyond this present life there will be no possibility of sinning if we are in Christ.

This present life is not only one of probation for mankind in general but for all believers also. The Christian's heavenly reward in the end will be related to his obedience to God's Word here and now. Hence some believers will receive greater reward than others. All will receive heaven; but some will be higher in heaven than others. 'Behold', cries our Saviour at the end of the Bible, 'I come quickly; and my reward is with me, to give every man according as his work shall be' (*Rev.* 22:12).

To live with one foot in the world may be pleasing to our corruptions. But it will take away from our eternal reward. To entertain strange doctrines may give us some popularity here. But it will take from our reward, for the fire will sweep away all chaff and all falsehood (*1 Cor.* 3:13). To live at ease in Zion when we might spend and be spent in the Master's service is gratifying to our carnality. But it will rob us of a 'full reward' (*2 John* 8). And once our probation is over we cannot recall it, nor repair the losses which our sins as converted Christians stole away from our measure of glory.

Then let us live with all our might for God while we do live.

24

The End of Time

Faith is a strange thing. As believers we have it; but not always in the same degree or in the same lively exercise. The truth appears to be that we are always inclined to backslide in our faith just as in all our other graces. The practical effect of this habit of secret decline is that we think ourselves to have more faith than in fact we do. If we are tempted to doubt the reality of this daily decline we must test ourselves in terms of our fears and our worries. We believe the Bible, we say. But then why are we so full of anxiety when the least thing goes wrong? We trust God, we say. But where is this trust whenever some problem arises?

The mischief of sin is that it is more subtle than anything else in the world. In that respect it resembles the devil himself. Sin leads us to think more highly of our faith than the facts warrant. Hence we take it for granted that we believe and are motivated by faith when in fact we are but weak in faith and more than half filled with doubt and unbelief. If we were to be given regular progress reports by the angels on the state of our faith we should no doubt be mortified to discover that we do not normally reach fifty percent.

Part of the problem is that there is a greater gap between theory and practice than we imagine. For instance, we subscribe to an infallible Bible. That is the right starting point, of course. Those who do not start there have not made a start at all. Those who do not trust what the Word of God says are locked into a hopeless world of doubt and fear. But when by grace we come to confess the infallible Word as our rule and as our guide in life, we have not removed every obstacle to a life of perfect faith. There is the internal difficulty which we all have to face in ourselves. It is the dreadful realisation that we do not believe what we believe. At least, we do not live by the rule as we know we should. It was after all to believers that our Saviour said, 'O ye of little faith'.

We say these things with the thought in mind that at the end of time, evidently, believers will not be so vigilant as they ought to be. To us it is strange that our Lord Jesus Christ should have to forewarn us that, among even the wise virgins, 'They all slumbered and slept' (*Matt.* 25:5). They had oil in their vessels with their lamps. They were in the best sense ready for his coming. They were worthy to enter into the presence of the King at his appearing. But they were so far affected with the spirit of the age that they, even they, are found in a state of sleepiness. Their faith in the imminent return of the Bridegroom is weak. If there are signs of the times, they seem not to observe them. If there are prodigies from heaven, as the Scriptures would lead us to expect just before the end, these good men and women do not lay them to heart. Christ is apparently to come back to a world in which even the good will be half asleep. He himself put it in these challenging words: 'When the Son of man cometh, shall he find faith in the earth?' (*Luke* 18:8).

It must be good for faith to think often of the end of time. Otherwise the Bible would not refer to it so frequently. The Bible is given above all else to create and to increase faith in us as the people of God in this world. Its teachings are so ordered and its visions so constructed that it is a perfect vehicle for generating and augmenting faith in the hearts of the saints.

Since this is so it is no surprise that the Bible should tell us so much or refer so many times to the great end which this world's history is to have. We should all of us be immersed in this world's pleasures if we did not know through the Word of God that an end is soon to be put to everything in this present order. Faith however tells the believer that there is no logic in living for the present. If in a few short years all that we see and all that we hear is to be swept away in the billows of God's wrath then we must gird up the loins of our minds and be sober. Faith informs the soul that the worldly life is madness and that those who are living the worldly life are living in a fool's paradise.

The view which the Scriptures give us of the end of the world is awesome in every way. For one thing the end will come to a society which is totally unprepared for it. This is not the same as saying that it will come to a society that is without warning of its approach. As we hinted earlier, there are passages of Scripture which indicate that there will be signs before the end of the world even as there were signs before the end of the Jewish state prior to its overthrow in A.D. 70. But such signs and warnings as God will give will go largely unheeded. Men will be eating and drinking, buying and selling, building and planting, marrying and giving in marriage, just as ever they have done in other times of history. The end of time will come upon the earth 'as a snare', warns our Lord (*Luke* 21:35).

That is to say, it will be unlooked for and unexpected. It will arrest them and stop them in their tracks as they are going about the normal affairs of life. Even as a beast is caught in a trap while travelling along its familiar paths and through its well-known hunting ground, so will the last day suddenly catch the wicked and drag them before the tribunal of the Almighty. It will occur in an instant and its consequences will be catastrophic and forever.

O what a vision the Bible presents to our gaze as we read of the great and dramatic end which our Maker has ordained for the history of his world! The last trumpet will sound. Earth's polluted atmosphere will be rent with a shrill blast whose volume will drown all other sounds. All symphonies of music will fall silent. All choirs of men will be hushed at the dread final clarion from earth's Creator. No more the sound of the mill or of the factory.

There will be no more heard the grinding of corn or the manufacture of metal goods. No more the hammer of the forge or the purring of the motor car. History's last sound will be not man-made but God-given. All televisions will fall silent. Their programmes will come to an abrupt conclusion. The incessant noise of popular music will stop at long last. The sports arena will know no more its frenzied excitement. Gone forever will be these earthly things. The day of the Lord will have come at last.

Then, what events are to follow or at least to accompany this trumpet sound! Christ himself will appear on the clouds of heaven with all his holy angels. The saints, both live and dead, being raised up in glory, will rise to meet the Lord in the air. The graves of the wicked will give back the carcasses of those who have lived and died in sin. These will rise to everlasting contempt and to everlasting shame. Then will the wicked call on the mountains and the hills to cover them and to hide them from the face of the Lord Jesus Christ as he comes to execute final judgement. Death will be preferred to life by the haters of God in that hour.

It is amazing what low views of God are entertained by the sinner. The present writer recalls once visiting a home where a husband, not a believer, had suddenly lost his wife while undergoing surgery. On seeing a minister of the gospel at his door attempting to comfort him, he exploded with the words: 'Wait till I see God. I will tell him what I think of him for taking my wife from me in this way!'

'O my dear friend', I said, 'I assure you that when you see your Maker you will not have any such thoughts as these!'

But such thoughts as those *are* in the sinner's heart in this life. He has exceedingly low and mean ideas of God and of the respect due to him. God is judged to be weak and contemptible by the ungodly man now in this life because men suppose him to be like themselves – careless of morals and irreverent in his nature. Men curse him regularly and with ease therefore. It is gratifying to the godless man to take the sacred Name in vain. Doing so has a ring of excitement. It is part of the thrill and pleasure of sinning for men to talk about their almighty Judge as if they could take him in their hands.

All such light thoughts of God will come to an abrupt end when men have to face him at the judgement seat, however. They will there realise that their worst fears respecting his holiness and righteousness were but too true and that he is infinite in purity and perfection. With a universal groan evil men and scoffers will see their Judge take down from its place the Book in which all their earthly lives are recorded. There will then be not a word or a deed but what they will have to answer strictly for.

With what confusion will the blasphemer, who but a short while ago profaned God with every tenth word, hear his own blasphemies read back to him in a long and fearful catalogue! With what irony of justice will the irreligious man feel the force of God's reproof: 'When they knew God they glorified him not as God neither were thankful' (*Rom.* 1:21)! All sinners will then see that they were fools to have preferred the praise that comes of men to the praise that comes from God only. Their own consciences will tell them that they are guilty and that they deserve the wrath that now awaits them eternally. Their excuses will appear to themselves to be futile and their refuges of lies will fail them.

In the same hour will the angels go out to gather out of all the earth the persons who have caused offence or who have worked wickedness in the whole earth. All these sinners will be bound in bundles to be burned. So there will be bundles of liars and bundles of murderers. Like with like, they will go together into the furnace of fire. As they loved their own vice, so their reward will be to be damned with those of the same vice. They will have the misery of being eternally in the close company of those who hated others in the same way as themselves.

O who can tell the woes of the damned or calculate their agonies in the lake of sulphurous flame? In vain will the damned long that they had never been born. In vain will they bewail their exile in the blackness of darkness, and in the place of eternal torment. 'Abandon hope, all ye who enter here' will be inscribed on their own consciousness. Hell moreover will be a worsening state in which men ever go further down into the bottomless pit. Since the damned in hell will sin eternally so, alas, they suffer ever increasing punishment as a reward of their wickedness. In this life God defers the punishment of sin till after men are dead. Sin is not punished for some time afterwards. But in hell there is no more divine forbearance. There is no more deferment of punishment. Sin, we must suppose, will be punished at once, as soon as it is committed. And it is being committed all the time. There are no words in existence to describe the lot of those sad souls who enter the inferno.

At the same time there will be marvellous sights at the end which will bring no less of delight and gladness to the righteous than the things mentioned above will bring of misery to the lost. The Saviour himself will appear, full of love for all his saints. As the great Shepherd he will gather his flock and lift his lambs into his bosom. So he will gently lead them, every single one of them, into the paradise of God. Not one will be forgotten or left behind. New heavens and a new earth will emerge in which there will be nothing offensive or vile. No creature there will ever hurt or destroy in all God's holy mountain. The city whose streets are all paved with gold will loom into the sight of the redeemed. They will enter in with shouts of victory and with songs of praise to the Lamb who loved them and died for them.

The elect will obtain joy and gladness, and sorrow and sighing will flee away, for God their Father will wipe away all tears from off their faces. Faith will now be rewarded with a sight of the breathtaking glories of the Triune God himself. Angelic choirs will accompany them home after their night of tribulation. Anthems of everlasting music will fill the rapturous hearts of all the people of God. Now is heaven to begin at last and the feast to be enjoyed which their Father promised them in Christ before the world began.

It is according to our faith in this heavenly vision that we shall labour for Christ in this present age. It is a sense of the imminence of these events that has led Christians in all ages, both men and women, to leave all and to follow the Lamb.

Here is the explanation for the way in which good people have in every age been ready to lay down their lives and to die to this world or else to expire in the service of others. Faith in these coming events, unseen as they are, is all-determinative of our present life and labour.

What an honour it is from Christ that he has told us so clearly that the end of all things is at hand! Some doctrines are not so clear or so plain to us in Scripture. But this is crystal clear. The day of the Lord draws near with every tick of the clock. The Judge is even now at the doors and his reward is with him. The night is far spent; the day is at hand. In a little while he will come whose right it is to sit on the throne of his father David. He will leave nothing at loose ends. Every act of service and love done for his sake will receive its due reward.

With these promises before the eye of our faith let us go forward in the duties of each new day.

25

Soon to See Jesus

Well did a recent and much-esteemed minister of the gospel entitle his book on the Second Coming of Christ 'The Momentous Event'! Momentous indeed will be that day when our great God-Man Redeemer appears on the clouds of heaven to call a halt to time and to bring down the curtain on earth's tortuous history. It will be an event of such magnitude for us all that we do well to make it the subject of our frequent meditation and our daily preparation. Indeed, our entire life ought to be little more than one long grooming of the soul for our introduction into Christ's majestic presence. Those happy children of earth who then find acceptance with him will lose all troubles and gain all joys; those, however rich here below, who fail in that last interview of all will lose all joys and spend eternity bewailing their unending losses.

An unearthly awe must possess our thoughts whenever we call to mind the momentous fact of Christ's Second Coming. It is the terminus at which all the saints have looked as, down the centuries, they have kept vigil here below. Deeply felt emotions stir the hearts of God's people as they wait and work and watch, knowing with the passing of every year and the rotation of every season that 'the night is far spent and the day is at hand' (*Rom.* 13:12). Grace gives instincts to believers and one of our instincts is to know that nothing matters in this world like the being right with God at the end of history. Here on earth many talk piously and many more scorn piety. But the intuition of a child of God has always been to look beyond false religion and irreligion, to that 'great and terrible day of the Lord' when the all-seeing eye of King Jesus will look with burning scrutiny into the secret recesses of every man's heart and life.

There are sensations in our heart when we think of Christ's return which are fraught with profoundest wonder. This is so first of all because of the nature of his Person. Our history knows of a multitude of kings and of great men. But here is now to appear at last the King of kings. When Jesus stands visibly upon the sky all eyes will see that this is *superlative* majesty. His is an essential and transcendent lordship, not inherited from his ancestors but his by virtue of Sonship within the ontological Trinity and his by decree of the Father in the everlasting covenant. The King who enters on the stage at our world's great finale is to be one whose presence will invest the name of monarchy with new lustre and beside whom all other kings will look and feel mere beggars.

But then too the coming of this God-Man fills us even now with awe because his appearing will be accompanied with alterations to the present order of things which are dreadful to contemplate. His hand will sweep aside the heavens and scatter the stars; his breath will extinguish the sun like a candle; his command will cause every mountain and island, every continent and ocean to vanish away like smoke. These shall be no longer. Now shall come the long-predicted hour when man's probation is over for ever and his day of accounting come. Not any more is to be heard the din of traffic, the bustle of commercial activity, the song of the drunkard, the peal of the wedding bell, the din of war or the shout of victory. These and all such things are over now and they will never begin to exist again to all eternity. When Jesus comes the game of sin is up, the sinner's dream is over. Reality, God and judgement must now be faced by all mankind at last.

It will be exquisite misery to the unbelieving portion of our world at Christ's coming to discover that the One who is now come is the One whom *they* crucified. Little did men suppose when they rejected and pierced him (as all Christ-haters virtually do every hour) that the Jesus of Nazareth whom they crucified was the eternal Jehovah come in disguise! Not for nothing did our Saviour identify himself to the Sanhedrin with these apocalyptic words: 'Hereafter shall ye see the Son of man sitting on the right hand of power, and coming in the clouds of heaven' (*Matt.* 26:64). Doubtless all sinners will guess his identity when the Saviour appears 'in the air' to be seen by 'every eye'. The Scripture makes it plain that they will then look on him whom they 'pierced' (*Rev.* 1:7). Jesus, so meek and mild in this day of grace, will be, and will be seen to be, of all possible enemies the very worst. There is no anger like the anger of a meek and gentle man when once he is roused to indignation. There will be nothing in all the catalogues of human anger to compare with what the Bible calls so ominously 'the wrath of the Lamb' (*Rev.* 6:16).

Some inkling of a coming Judgement Day is to be found among even heathen nations. The Greeks and Romans certainly had some very clear notions on that subject, whether learnt from conscience or from their remote ancestry – or perhaps by second-hand acquaintance with the Jewish Scriptures. But no pagan thought ever reached the height of foreseeing that mankind's Judge would be its Saviour and its God-incarnate. These sublime mysteries are to be gleaned only from the Word of God and they invest the coming of our Lord with peculiar poignancy and power.

How wise it was of God to place upon the seat of Judgement One who is a man and a sufferer at men's hands, as all his people have been! No bold sinner can ever hurl at his dread Judge the accusation that he does not know what it is to be tempted, to feel pain or to face death. For Jesus has felt all this and endured it sinlessly. The sinner before the bar of 'the man Christ Jesus' will be 'speechless'. His own conscience will inform him that he has no cloak for his sin – especially not for his sin of refusing the free pardon offered to him while in this life. Men may despise a gentle Saviour now; but they will rue it eternally when once he steps down to sit on the Judgement seat and summons them to look him in the eye.

O how wasteful of precious time is our poor, foolish world! Day passes after day. Year follows year. So the centuries go by. Yet men grow no wiser in their use of time. Each moment of our earthly life affords us all a golden opportunity for repentance and reconciliation with God. Week after week, Sabbath after graciously-given Sabbath, Christ and the cross are preached to mankind as the one and only way to heaven. Given the brevity of life and of all human time, one would expect to see whole streets of men, whole cities – indeed, whole continents of men – hurrying to press into Christ's kingdom while yet the door stands open. But the mass of men pass ever onwards towards the great Last Day as heedless of the impending hour of Christ's coming today as they were in Noah's day. 'History teaches that history teaches nothing.' Not one in a thousand spends ten seconds in a day preparing for this coming 'momentous event'! 'There is a way that *seems* right unto a man.' So begins a famous Proverb. 'But the end thereof are the ways of *death*' (*Prov.* 14:12). It *seems* right to men to follow one another in their pursuit of earthly wealth and pleasure. It *seems* right to live only for today; to leave tomorrow's reckoning till we get there; to hope that 'our luck will be in' when health and life run out and when we too must grapple with eternity, as all the generations before us have had to do.

But this is the sure way to *death* – to that 'second death' from which there is to be no escape. No man ever tumbled into heaven by accident. No man will find himself worthy of eternal life who did not in this life exert himself to find Christ and to be his disciple. The happy-go-lucky man is, in the things of God, a lost man. They who now fear nothing, not even the Lord's return, will one day discover that they have only postponed their fears. A sinner's fears are coming to meet him fast. His death will be a double death when it comes. For when a careless sinner dies he has nothing ahead of him but cares. A Christless man's eternity will be one long, unbroken midnight of fear.

O that the nearness of Christ's return might be a fact engraved upon the consciousness of every Christian! O that every preacher would have this truth etched as with a pen of iron and the point of a diamond upon the table of his heart! Our time for witnessing and for preaching is fast ebbing away. Souls are flying every moment into the great eternity beyond time. When once the Master rises up and beckons to the attendant angel, the trumpet of doom will sound and men's destinies will be fixed forever in heaven or else in hell. It would be a wholesome exercise for every preacher daily to recall the Saviour's words: 'The night cometh, when no man can work' (*John* 9:4).

The coming of Christ will be no less momentous for good to God's people than it will be for ill to the wicked. The picture presented to us in God's Word is beautiful and comforting in the extreme. As the cockerel heralds the coming of the new day, so will the trumpet's blast announce the endless, joyous, cloudless day of everlasting redemptive glory for the sons of God. At last the Jubilee will come. The long, dark night of sorrow will be ended for the saints. Jesus himself will put his head out of heaven to call them up higher. Like a cloud the ransomed of the Lord will rise up into the air to meet him at his coming whom they have loved and lived for here on earth. 'This is our God, we have waited for him' will be their universal anthem (*Isa.* 26:8).

As by a hidden magnetism, the power of Christ will lift up to himself all and only those who are his. There will be two in a bed, in the field, at the work place. 'One shall be taken and the other left' (*Luke* 17:34–36). Election and the covenant promise will mean everything to men then, when those whom God has loved and washed in the blood of Christ are marshalled before the face of King Jesus in the air.

Exquisite and ineffable will be the comforting sense of privilege which the redeemed will know at this momentous event. What a world of bliss it will be to each lowly Christian to hear the Master call him by name and bid him welcome forever into His loving presence! 'Fear not: for I have redeemed thee. I have called thee by thy name; thou art mine', will Christ say to them (*Isa.* 43:1).

Let every tired Christian in this busy, secular age often recall the mighty truth of Christ's momentous return. Often let him pause to refresh his spirit with this hope: 'Soon we shall see Jesus!'

26

The Christian's Posthumous Joy

We may not often stop to say why it is so, but we all feel that the saying is true: 'He that laughs last, laughs best.' This proverb strikes the mind as fair because it suggests that, until the end of the story comes, the wrong people have been laughing and those who are worthy to laugh have been kept from doing so because of their sad circumstances. But once the story comes to its last chapter and the good receive what they have waited for, then *they* laugh. The laughter of their enemies may have been long and loud; but it did not last. On the other hand, the tears of the righteous may have been many and bitter; but in the final chapter they are wiped away. So much is intimated by the familiar saying of which we speak.

This proverb is a paraphrase of half the Bible's teaching. From one end of the Word of God to the other we find its message to be this: laughter and joy to God's children in the end. The other half of its message of course is the reverse: sorrow and weeping in the end to the wicked. The point to which we draw attention here is that the Christian's laughter is his *last* experience. Others may enjoy laughter and mirth occasionally, perhaps frequently, along the brief journey of this present life. But they will not be those who 'laugh last'.

Christians, and none but they, will 'laugh last' – and so they will 'laugh best'.

It is evident that the above view of the matter is that of the Lord Jesus Christ and of all his faithful servants in both Old Testament and New. 'Blessed are ye that weep now: for ye shall laugh', says our Saviour (*Luke* 6:21). On the other hand, the same Lord adds: 'Woe unto you that laugh now! for ye shall mourn and weep' (*Luke* 6:25). In similar fashion Isaiah had before cried to Israel of old: 'Say ye to the righteous, that it shall be well with him: for they shall eat the fruit of their doings. Woe unto the wicked! it shall be ill with him: for the reward of his hands shall be given him' (*Isa.* 3:10–11). Similarly the apostle John, with great vividness of expression, declares: 'Reward her even as she rewarded you, and double unto her double according to her works: in the cup which she hath filled, fill to her double. How much she hath glorified herself and lived deliciously, so much torment and sorrow give her' (*Rev.* 18:6–7). Clearly, the righteous had not had much of a laughing time while the wicked were in power. But now their positions are reversed by the Second Coming of Christ. These passages of Scripture are typical of many more to the same effect.

The teaching which we find in such Scriptures as the above must surely be instructive and comforting. This present world is, and always has been for God's children, a difficult place. So long as error and falsehood are on the world's throne, we must expect truth and righteousness to be pilloried and placed on the scaffold. This is not to deny that there are joys along the way to heaven. But we must expect them to be much marred by the inward pain which we feel at the presence of countless evils. Perhaps a great part of our sanctification consists in our progressively learning by experience that this world is to us an alien planet and must be so viewed by us till Christ renews it at his glorious appearing. Till Christ our Redeemer comes on the clouds we must make up our minds to expect this to be a world where all the wrong people are laughing.

It is easy to put it like that in cold print. But it is no easy thing to keep calm while passing through the actual experience of it. There is, after all, a spirit in man. We do not find it easy to see error and indiscipline in the house of God. Yet we are forced to see it very extensively there. Our gorge rises when we hear of it and when we see it. Similarly, we do not find it an easy thing to stand by while liberal politicians bulldoze away the Christian principles which once made our nations safe places to live in and, at least in some periods of the past, places where the gospel flourished. It is no easy thing for God's children to witness the rise of drug addiction, violence, divorce and irreligion in towns and cities where once sin was ashamed to open its mouth.

The Christian's greatest joys are reserved for the world to come. Those which he experiences here on earth are wonderful enough. But they by no means match the superior comforts and triumphs which await him hereafter. It is for this reason that all Christians believe that the best joys will be on the farther side of the grave and in eternity. Our laughing time will then coincide with the world's crying time. It cannot come till the mask is torn off from the face of the spirit who now deceives the nations. In that day Satan will be seen to be the arch-liar and the chief promoter of history's long pantomime of deceit. From the very beginning God's people have declared this to be so. But this message has been scorned by a world which loves to believe in a fool's paradise.

Once a believer enters eternity he will have nothing but a rising tide of comforts and pleasures. His prayers and service will bring him posthumous joy.

Take the example of a Christian father and mother. They brought up their children in this world in the ways of God. But both died before they heard of the salvation of any of their family. Their children, we may say, brought down their parents' 'grey hairs with sorrow to the grave' (*Gen.* 42:38). To all outward appearance the parents' labour of love was lost. Their sons and daughters saw no need of God or of the Saviour. With a sigh both parents closed their eyes at death on a family whose only 'religion' was worldly pleasure.

Imagine then their joy in the glory of the upper world to see their once rebellious children coming one by one to Zion! Picture their ecstasy as they hear the story of how a Holy Spirit graciously and sovereignly arrested them with the recollection, years after their parents' death, of truths taught by them and exemplified in their lives. What happy posthumous joy!

Take a different example. Let us suppose a poor mother in England during the Middle Ages. God had opened her eyes by some means to see the superstition of the church in her day. With inward sighs she sees how ignorantly the people around her venerate their saints, pray to the Virgin, adore the wafer, confess sin to the priest. It is clear to her that the vast bulk of her parish – not to say, of the whole land – are going to hell 'with a lie in their right hand' (*Isa.* 44:20). She prays to God for the church, for the land and for a brighter day to dawn upon the whole world. But she lives to see not a spark of that glorious Reformation which is to come.

Picture then her posthumous joy when at the last day she is informed that her many prayers on earth came up 'for a memorial before God' (*Acts* 10:4). In answer to her lifelong yearning for revival, God had given her a male descendant – John Wycliffe by name – who was like the 'morning star' to all the world. In due course the light of the gospel broke out which she vainly sought on earth, not over the British Isles only but over all Europe and mankind! Not in this brief life here below, surely, are we to discover that God answers prayer 'exceeding abundantly above all that we could ask or even think' (*Eph.* 3:20).

Again, we offer a further illustration. A Christian writer toils away daily at his desk prayerfully attempting to turn the blank sheets of paper in front of him into edifying books and articles to strengthen his beloved brethren in their precious ministries. We refer, of course, to such a writer as the late A.W. Pink. Pressing on with the task day by day and year by year – often against ill health, fatigue and shortage of time – he finishes his course at last and lays down his burden at the close of life. Yet here below he sees no great movement of the Spirit of God; he hears of no significant change in the life of the visible church; he is aware of only small interest world-wide in his own work.

Picture then his posthumous joy when, on the Last Day, he is informed of the many thousands of hungry souls who fed in after years upon his writings. Imagine his rejoicing to hear that they corrected their imperfect theology by studying his books and lit good gospel lights in many parts of the world as a result of reading what he painfully and tearfully had written. It is not in this life only that the people of God are to realise the truth of the Scripture which tells us that 'the Word of God is not bound' (*2 Tim.* 2:9).

The illustrations of this principle – so it seems to us – can be multiplied endlessly. The good which good men do is not always a source of great joy to them here and now in this life. Here 'all things are full of labour' (*Eccl.* 1:8). Even the sweetest duty of all, prayer and communion with God, is in this life at times marred by our bodily fatigue and by our mental weariness. But 'God is not unrighteous to forget' (*Heb.* 6:10) the loving services of his devoted people. Most of what Christians do for Christ now is quickly forgotten by them. On the Last Day, however, Christ will take pleasure in reminding his servants of all that they have done. He will not overlook a 'cup of cold water' given for his sake (*Matt.* 10:42). The warm handshake to the preacher at the church door by an appreciative hearer and the quiet word of encouragement to one who is faithful in the work yet weary in it – these things will be rewarded posthumously by the Lord Jesus in the Day when the books are opened (*Rev.* 20:12).

It must not be supposed that we intend any unkindness to lost sinners when we say that the Christian will laugh best when he laughs last. As Christians, we do not grudge the world any innocent pleasure now. Nor do we inwardly resent whatever good things God may see fit to give to unbelievers in this life.

The sad truth is, however, that Christless men and women spoil their own blessings by not thanking God for them. Because they love 'the creature more than the Creator' (*Rom.* 1:25) they show that their 'mind and conscience are defiled' (*Titus* 1:15). So they suffer the sad judgement by which in this life God 'curses their blessings' (*Mal.* 2:2) and makes their worldly good to be 'a snare and a trap and a stumbling block' to them (*Psa.* 69:22). This is a righteous judgement because evil men are 'unthankful' and 'unholy' (*2 Tim.* 3:2) even in the midst of their highest earthly comforts and favours.

On the other hand, as the people of God we are taught to wait patiently for our good things since we know that if we 'suffer with Christ' in this life, 'we shall also reign with him' in the life to come (*2 Tim.* 2:12).

It is a sign that Christians have backslidden whenever they are impatient for their good things and begin to demand them *in this life*. The professing Christian who casts a wistful glance towards the public house or the dance hall or the night-club has forgotten that all these things belong to the world which is 'enmity with God' (*Jas.* 4:4). There *are* lawful joys for the Christian here in this life. But we must take heed that we do not venture on to the enchanted ground of sensual joys. The end of such things is 'death' (*Rom.* 6:21) and it is deeply to be regretted that in our age the gap between the church and the world is becoming perilously narrow.

If ever we forget that our best joys are those which we are to have with Christ beyond this life, we have taken the first step to losing them. Those Christians who, like Lot, 'pitch their tent towards Sodom' (*Gen.* 13:12) by living as close to the world as they dare, will not increase their happiness in the end but greatly diminish it. Surely M'Cheyne was not wrong when he reminded Christians that sins committed after conversion take away from their eternal reward.

It is a strange 'evangelical' religion which leaves those who profess it little wiser in their choice of pleasures and pastimes than the unbeliever. Let the children of this world, if they must, find their delight in lusts, excess of wine, revellings (*1 Pet.* 4:3) and questionable entertainments. Such things scarcely belong to the lifestyle of those who profess to have been born into God's family and who claim to be the disciples of the apostles and of the Reformers. Those who secretly love the world really belong to it (*1 John* 4:5).

Professing Christians who find their delight in worldly pleasures are, according to God's Word, 'dead while they live' (*1 Tim.* 5:6) and may discover in the grave that in their case there is to be no such thing as posthumous joy. Many, perhaps all, who come into this class will hear the doleful words: 'Son, remember that thou in thy lifetime receivedst thy good things' (*Luke* 16:25). The implication is that they had them *all* here. They are to have no others. Solemn words with which to begin one's life in eternity!

The age in which we live is a time of testing and of sifting. Because that is so, the true Christian must be prepared for a few discouragements and disappointments in the meantime. False faith grows impatient in such times and looks for an opportunity to cast off the fear of God. But true faith preserves those who have it because it knows what others do not really know, that a believer's best blessings are beyond the grave. No Christian ever lost anything by shunning sin or worldly pleasure. Today we are to work in the vineyard; very soon we shall drink with Christ the royal wine of heaven.

FAITHFULNESS IN THE
MODERN CHURCH

27

Cleansing the Lord's House

The most important spiritual issues which we face as Christians and as churches are inevitably the most painful ones. That is why they are seldom addressed with real earnestness by any but a few. It is much easier to leave the vital question unasked and the sore point unprobed so that no one is offended and no one is embarrassed. In the secular world this is called 'sweeping things under the carpet', and it has to be admitted that the metaphor is a good one. Things swept under a carpet are out of sight, and they are therefore easily forgotten by everyone who happens to be living and working in the room. Things swept under a carpet are nuisances, but they are nuisances not easily noticed by visitors, and that is one substantial point in their favour.

There are, however, some solid disadvantages to the practice of sweeping rubbish under church rugs. For one thing, the rubbish does not go away. It stays there till someone with a little more moral courage – perhaps the next minister, or a conscientious deacon – is bold enough to point his finger at it and suggest something be done. Woe betide him, however, if he is not wearing armour plating when the ammunition starts to fly! He almost certainly was not the original cause of the compromise himself, but merely pointing out the problem is enough to make him in the eyes of many to be 'the troublemaker'. All who knew and approved of the cover-up will now be sure to turn on him with tones of injured innocence. 'Why', say these sour saints, 'did you have to expose all that?' So covering up the dust with the rug has this disadvantage, that it lays a trap in the long run for the most honest members of the congregation. The innocent are charged with the blame of others' sins by merely mentioning them.

More serious still, rubbish under church mats may remain out of sight to most visitors, but it can never be out of sight to the one Visitor whose presence is all-important. Is it not amazing how inconsistent we can be? At one moment we expound the doctrine of God's omniscience; at the next we act in matters of church practice as if God were blind to our deviousness. We talk volumes about the Holy Spirit; but we can be stone deaf to 'what the Spirit saith unto the churches' (*Rev.* 2:7). If these epistles early in the Book of Revelation teach anything, they surely teach us that Jesus Christ does not dwell for very long in churches where sin is left undealt with.

It is surprising – not to say alarming – what things can lie dormant under church mats until they are brought to light by the all-seeing eye of Christ. Church mats may be beautifully woven with eloquent theology and vibrant singing, with the logo of seeming orthodoxy and the fringe of a specious faithfulness. But all that, if these epistles are the standard to judge by, is no guarantee that there may not be, underneath the surface, a volume of nastiness: lack of love, perhaps; or a deal of morally questionable behaviour, or a mere 'name to live' and nothing more than the name; or even, in some instances, a nauseating lukewarmness.

The attitude which tries to cover up sin among saints is both misguided and dangerous. It is misguided because it wrong-headedly puts the feelings of men before the honour of Christ. In an effort to spare a few guilty sinners the pain of exposure, confession and repentance, this attitude would prefer to leave sin uninvestigated and undisciplined. But the price to be paid is expensive. It may place the whole church or congregation under the angry frown of Christ. He usually gives to churches a space to repent. But if they shirk their duty by choosing the easy option of turning a blind eye to known sin, they can expect Christ's rod to fall on their back. When the space given to act righteously is not taken by those in authority, Christ's patience will come to an end. Unhappy the church where this happens! Grace and peace soon vanish. Love takes wings and flies off. The upshot is pandemonium in the pulpit and in the pew. Tongues and tempers are let loose and let fly. Soon the old saying becomes visibly true: 'There is no trouble like church trouble.'

There are good practical reasons why the whole theme of church discipline needs to be looked at everywhere in these days. For one thing, it has much to do with the burning question of why there is so little blessing in so many churches today. If we are not mistaken, this is a fact and a very painful one. It is a fact which cannot be wished away, however we might try. It is a disagreeable and stubborn fact that many orthodox churches are seeing very few conversions, very little holy enthusiasm and very little impact on the outside world. Why this is so we do not presume to understand. But it should not escape our notice that churches may be faithful to Christ in one sense and yet be unfaithful to him in another. By this we mean that a church may be theoretically and constitutionally faithful, yet at the same time practically and really disobedient to Christ. It may be more disobedient, indeed, than a doctrinally weaker church.

An example or two may help to make the point clear. Let us suppose there is a congregation in a town which swears unqualified submission to the Bible as the Word of God, which subscribes to Calvinistic articles of faith, and which has a high theory of preaching and of public worship. Down the street is another church where less theology is known and understood. Yet it is possible for the second church to have a greater faithfulness to Christ than the first in a number of ways.

It may be a sad but undeniable fact that the elders and minister of the first church do not examine candidates for church membership half so thoroughly as does the second church. They may tolerate greater laxity in personal and family life. They may never really challenge the consciences of the unconverted. They may not be half so regular at the meetings for Bible study or prayer. They may timidly neglect to warn the unruly and to rebuke carelessness in life and practice.

What comment does the above, all too possible, scenario call for? What conclusion are we to draw? Surely this: that Arminian churches put us to shame if they actively promote holiness in their members, carefully examine prospective communicants, discipline the unruly member and show diligence in their attendance on the means of grace – whilst we in Calvinistic churches do not. Our theory is better than theirs. But if it is unpractised theory, it is hardly going to commend us to God for being theory which is better on paper but not in application.

Similarly, if the Arminian church along the street, whose doctrine and theory are weaker than ours, practises a realistic application of gospel principles to the lives of its people, is it not at that level doing more to honour Christ than the sounder church mentioned earlier? In our view it is. Their Arminianism is, in one or two practical respects, putting our 'Calvinism' in the shade. Or rather, should we not say that our Calvinism is become a sort of un-Calvinism, much in the same way as Paul puts it when he tells the decadent Jews that their 'circumcision' is become 'uncircumcision' (Rom. 2:25)?

The above example is, of course, invented purely for the purpose of illustrating the point under consideration. It is fervently to be hoped that Calvinistic churches never commit the sort of gross neglect we have referred to. But the possibility is there, to say the least. Of course, such a theoretical 'Calvinism' would never be owned by the John Calvin of history, whose firm faithfulness as a pastor made him ready to suffer exile. Doubtless, too, he would have gladly undergone death had this been the price required of him for his duty to Christ.

Let no one mistake what we are arguing for when we speak of faithful church discipline. We have no wish to be associated with any heavy-handed form of 'shepherding' nor with an intrusive or bullying attitude towards the people of God. The historic view of church discipline is that which safeguards gospel principle in the lives of professing Christians and no more. It does not attempt to lord it over God's heritage. It knows nothing about dictating to church members as to whom they will marry (except 'in the Lord'), or what house they must buy or where they shall go for their holidays. One occasionally hears of such types of disciplinary rigidity as these which, by stepping over the line of Scripture, make fear of man, not love to Christ, the primary restraint. But there is a more perfect way.

Discipline, however, must not be left simply to mean the following of formalised procedures. A faithful ministry must anticipate problems and attempt to avoid the worst things happening by taking pre-emptive measures. If a brother or a sister is visibly backsliding, in other words, wise oversight will give a word of warning before slipping has become slipping away. What else can the Word of God mean when it tells us to 'exhort one another daily . . . lest any . . . be hardened through the deceitfulness of sin' (*Heb.* 3:13)?

The formal process of discipline is the last resort. When the last resort is appropriate – that is to say, when serious sin has been committed – sentence of suspension, or even of excommunication, is to be passed upon the offender. It is never easy for the church to do this. But where it is the only form of censure appropriate to the gravity of the scandal committed, it is a church's duty to proceed without timidity. The failure to censure, when scandalous sin is proved to have been committed, is treason to Christ.

The title of this article refers to our constant and continual duty to keep pure the church of God. It is a perpetual problem, and no church can afford to be indifferent to it if it is to expect God's blessing. The ideal is for all the membership, from the pastor to the people, to study holiness by vigilance, prayer and mortification of sin. This way is the most painless in the long run. The seat of the problem, after all, is not in the fellowship but in the human heart. Where saints make conscience of keeping short accounts with God, they will hardly and seldom need to experience the rigours of formal church discipline. Those who tremble at God's voice and so fear to offend his Holy Spirit will not often need to be cited to appear before the eldership to answer formal charges of serious indiscipline.

The aim of the gospel ministry must be to build churches which are as pure as by grace we can make them. Our Calvinism is to find expression in our observance of biblical principles in the context of the congregation's overall service to Christ. All is not done when sound sermons are preached. Sound preaching requires as its corollary sound living and, although sound living is not angelic perfection, it is a meaningful obedience to Christ's revealed will.

The need to cleanse and keep cleansed the house of God has a bearing on that master problem of our day and age, our lack of power in preaching. There is evidence in the Word of God to suggest that the measure of our power is related to the measure of our spirituality and of our church purity. It would be wrong to connect these two things too minutely, as if pure churches were always bound to experience revival. But the stubborn fact faces us today that something is grieving the Spirit and restraining the longed-for visitation. Could it be that we have lost our savour of holiness as churches?

If, in the matter of church reform, we do what we can, it may be that God will, in the matter of revival, do for us what we cannot. Certainly we have need of him to make our churches what they frequently are not, so that the world outside may believe.

28

Christ's Unshepherded Sheep

If we are not mistaken, there are growing numbers of unhappy Christians in our Western world. Their unhappiness is not the result of a natural awkwardness or temperamental discontentedness, but of a dissatisfaction with what is being offered to them in their home churches in the name of worship and preaching. Our heart goes out to them in deep compassion. They deserve a special mention and ought to have a regular place in our prayers.

Over the past three decades so many winds of doctrine have blown through the churches that they may be said with justification to have reached gale-force proportions. But the problem does not end with doctrine. It extends to forms and styles of public worship. If the rumours which reach our ears are anywhere near the mark it would seem that half the churches which were once sound and evangelical have entered second childhood. Often the only qualification worshippers need to get accreditation from their leaderships is to be able to wave their arms about like the fronds of a palm tree and to be reasonably fluent at speaking gibberish. The possession of a thinking mind is a positive disadvantage since it puts those who have it in the unenviable position of realising how ludicrous the whole affair is, and how unprofitable.

Churches in a panic

There must be several factors which have led once great and steadfast evangelical churches to decide for childish worship. One factor is the need which so many feel of catering for the young. By the 1960s and '70s it became apparent that the rising generation was becoming unchurched. The young were no longer drawn to church services by the good old habits of previous generations but were poisoned off the things of God by the popular music of their day and by the galloping influence of television and sport.

This obvious phenomenon caused many Christian leaders to agonise about their 'image' in the eyes of the young. It was no longer thought possible for Christian parents to discipline their families or to keep their children unspotted from the world. The fault, so it was said, was with the church itself. It was 'old-fashioned'. It lacked 'excitement' and 'appeal'. If young persons were to be kept, new and more lively styles of worship needed to be introduced. So the argument ran.

Without doubt, this type of reasoning led to a good deal of haste and unbelief. Leaders, in many cases with good motivation and yet with secret misgivings, handed over the conduct of church services to young people. Little by little, the panic spread. Gravity and order, once held to be virtues in the worship of the Almighty, now came to be pilloried as arch-enemies of spiritual worship. 'Freedom' and 'spontaneity' became the new norms of worship. After all, where the Spirit is there is freedom, and why should that freedom not be available to *all* to make use of? Away with the shackles that bound the former generations! Worship had at last come of age. Men, women and children must all be free to participate audibly and actively.

The results are with us at this day. The fruits of a general anarchy of worship are that noise replaces reverence and shallowness supplants spiritual maturity, while anything at all squeezes out the sermon. The typical worshipper, as one has said, might as well unscrew his head before the service begins because that part of his anatomy is irrelevant and might be left under the seat for all the use it is during a church service of this type.

Great harm to true saints

Our purpose in drawing attention to these evils is to attempt to show how harmful they are to the true flock of Christ. Those who have souls to be fed and do not just come to church mindlessly can only be alarmed and offended by such superficial worship. The child of grace knows God to be glorious in holiness. He comes to the house of God with reverence and fear. He is taught by the Spirit to have a high and reverent attitude to anything and everything that belongs to God's worship. He longs for the presence of God to be felt in the heart and for the truths of Scripture to be made plain and powerful to him in his mind. When he sees other worshippers excited by frothy and foolish nonsense, whether in the worship or the preaching, he is inwardly indignant. He is hurt because he knows the Spirit of the Lord is grieved.

This, alas, is just what is happening in churches of all sorts all around us. Serious believers who would die for Christ if called on to do so are in too many cases being made to feel unwelcome in their own congregations. Their spirituality is misinterpreted for awkwardness. The most mature Christians in the church are being made to feel isolated by their fellows because they cannot praise the cheery sing-along which others seem to crave in the name of 'worship'. In this way there has come about a situation in which the service of worship is often a test of patience rather than a time of devotion for the best of God's people. They do not want to cause trouble but their grieved consciences cannot approve the novel songs, the novel choruses, the novel mimes, the novel atmosphere in the place where they and their fathers once worshipped God with holy fear.

Spirituality at stake

This is not of course a question of mere age or generation. It is much rather a matter of spirituality, of maturity and of knowledge. There are older Christians who behave like children. Thankfully, too, there are also younger Christians who have made such good use of their Bibles, books and Confessions of Faith as already to be well-grounded and well-studied believers.

Spiritual people come to church to meet with God. They do not want to have entertainment intruded upon them. Those who desire entertainment may obtain it at any time from the many theatres and amusement halls where it is generously provided for worldly minds. There is a place for relaxation and for mirth of a pure and wholesome kind. God's people need to laugh at times as others do. Whilst they avoid worldly forms of amusement they do not refuse occasionally to be merry and light-hearted. But the people of God do not go to church for their entertainment. They do not seek amusement there nor do they relish finding it there. Worship and amusement never go together. Worship and entertainment never go together. Worship and levity never go together.

What is at stake in all of this is that precious thing which we call spirituality. The spiritual man trembles at God's Word and has a high view of every aspect of and element in God's worship. Not only does he require spirituality in the preaching. He requires and expects it in the reading of the Scriptures, in public prayer and in the content and tone of religious singing. He expects it in God's house and he has every right to find it there.

Spiritual loneliness

It is not difficult to see why so many of Christ's people today are lonely in the crowded gathering. They rejoice when the church is thronged with people. But they are troubled if they discover that there is nothing in the church but a noisy crowd. They are bound to wonder if perhaps after all a hundred serious worshippers – or even twenty-five – are not preferable to an irreverent multitude.

This must not be confused with a 'little flock' mentality. We do not applaud the theory that churches should always be small. On the contrary, they ought in our view to be very large. Churches of a thousand are, to our mind, not too large. We wish the land were full of them.

But numbers for numbers' sake is often treason to Christ. The leadership lowers the standard of holiness to attract the largest crowds. At a critical point in this process of dilution the worship ceases utterly to be recognisable as such by those who walk carefully with God. The crowd may grow but the spiritual and lonely Christian who witnesses the decline fears that the Spirit is withdrawn and gone. 'Ichabod' is the church's real name. Spiritual fellowship is almost impossible to find any more. The few really holy Christians left are isolated and lonely.

No loneliness is so hard to bear as loneliness in a crowd. How many Christians there are who feel this condition in their own churches! They are the last to speak of it because they are prayerful, patient and long-suffering. But it is no credit to their pastors and elders that this state of affairs has come about. By diluting the worship they have attracted in an uncertain multitude but they have made sad the hearts of the righteous.

Casualties of the change

There are visible casualties as a result of the kind of changes we have spoken of. One of these is the atrocious treatment occasionally meted out to faithful shepherds of the flock who refuse to change. Because they cannot in conscience go along with the general stampede to 'brighten' the worship of God, good ministers are having to leave their churches. It does not count that they have spent twenty or thirty years dutifully and faithfully opening up the Word of God to their flocks. Their crime is to be resistant to the universal cry for innovation. So our good men must go to make room for the menu of improvements insisted on by the youth leader and weak deacons.

Another and scarcely less ominous fruit of this new style of church life is the rise in our times of practical anti-nomianism. One shrinks from referring to it in any detail. But the fact is that new church worshippers are a lot less successful at resisting temptation than the old used to be. There may at times have been excess of severity in the older types of church service. But they were safe. They did not play about with temptation. They did not appeal to the flesh. People appeared in God's house in strictly proper dress and with consummate decorum. Alas, that cannot always be said of some more recent types of worship. A mixed multitude in God's house brings the whole level down. Every minister knows that there are too many moral casualties resulting from this lack of the practice of holiness. It ought not to be so.

It is a comfort to God's unshepherded sheep to know that they have in heaven a Shepherd who sees their state. They must remind themselves of their true position as their Shepherd portrays it in such a passage as Ezekiel 34. They are lonely because of the ineptitude and incompetence of their leaders. They are unloved and unwanted by men because they are too spiritual for their generation. But Christ will require from their neglectful shepherds an explanation for their neglect one day. Moreover Christ himself will take his despised and lonely people to himself, giving them his gracious presence here and his glorious presence hereafter.

What words for the lonely modern Christian to ponder are these: 'I will require my flock at their hand' (v.10); 'Behold I, even I, will both search my sheep, and seek them out' (v.11); 'I will deliver them out of all places where they have been scattered in the cloudy and dark day' (v.12); 'I will feed them in a good pasture; and upon the high mountains of Israel shall their fold be' (v.14); 'Behold, I judge between cattle and cattle, between the rams and the he goats' (v.17); 'I the Lord will be their God, and my servant David [Christ] a prince among them; I the Lord have spoken it' (v.24)!

With such promises, who would not be lonely with Christ for a time in this world?

29

Man Grasping to Be Superman

In a wonderful and familiar passage of the New Testament we read that Christ 'thought it not robbery to be equal with God' (*Phil.* 2:6). Translators and commentators help us to seize the precise meaning of this thought by suggesting that equality with God was not, for Christ, something 'to be grasped' or 'snatched at'. Our blessed Lord had equality with God and he never lost it. But he chose for our sakes to appear in this world in so humble a form that men supposed him not to be God.

Christ did not lay aside his godhood, but by taking our nature into union with himself he exposed himself, while on earth, to profound misunderstanding on the part of others. In that way he did not make a full display, as he had every right to do, of the divine godhead which was his. During the days of our Saviour's life on earth he appeared, as it were, in disguise. A veil covered his infinite and eternal glory – a veil which was not lifted in his earthly life except once, during the Transfiguration.

It should not escape our notice that in so acting Christ behaved in a manner quite the reverse of others. The self-effacement of the Son of God is in complete contrast to the grasping spirit which was the undoing of so many myriads of fallen angels and men. They strove to be and to appear higher and mightier than their created order had made them. Fallen creatures all fell over the same ambitious desire to be 'as gods' or, to put it another way, 'as God' (*Gen.* 3:5).

This was the glittering prize which seduced our first parents, and it is ominously similar to the aim and objective which had earlier ruined the Tempter: 'I will ascend into heaven, I will exalt my throne above the stars of God . . . I will ascend above the heights of the clouds; I will be like the most High' (*Isa.* 14:13–14). Satan, like Adam after him and like all Adam's children more or less since, set his 'heart as the heart of God' (*Ezek.* 28:6). It should not confuse us that in the prophetic passages where these statements appear they refer to the Kings of Babylon and Tyrus. *Their* grasping pride was the same as Adam's and it was no different from that of Satan or 'Lucifer, son of the morning' (*Isa.* 14:12).

It must strike us on serious reflection to be a strange thing that the only two orders of rational beings, angels and men, have both had an inclination to become God. It was not that they were badly done by in the condition in which God made them. On the contrary, they had everything they needed to make them happy. Satan once shined as a bright angel in the firmament of heaven. And our first parents had a perfect paradise with full permission to enjoy it. Only one restriction was put by God on their freedom. But it was one they could not bear. They followed the pattern of fallen angels in grasping what was not theirs by right. This history is well known. But we draw attention to the remarkable fact that one and the same fatal craving in angels and men led to the ruin of them both.

A philosopher might well find fertile soil for speculation in this curious circumstance to which we here refer. Is it in some way part of the mind of creatures to crave to be more than we are? Is it a case of the heart yearning to become what the eye sees? Is it the fascination which the created being has with the very idea of God? We do not pretend to know the answer to such questions. But the fact appears to be that there is in rational beings an appetite to become something bigger than we are. The evidence is in history and it is also right before our eyes in this proud world of ours where men aspire to be supermen.

It is a matter for profound thankfulness that the ambition of Satan to be God failed. It may do us no harm to imagine for a moment what life would be like if Satan could have succeeded. For the blessed God to be no longer ruler of the universe is the ultimate nightmare. To have to pray to Satan for our daily bread, for help, guidance, mercy and heaven – Oh what unutterable slavery! To have to spend eternity worshipping Satan – Oh what sevenfold spiritual torment! To look to the prince of evil for pity, grace and compassion – Oh what sublime disappointment! With unspeakable relief we return to the blessed thought that God alone rules the world. Our loving heavenly Father is the unrivalled monarch of the skies. It is the greatest mercy in all existence!

Man's unbelief is his own worst enemy. The torture of mind which men bring on themselves by unbelief is as tragic as it is senseless. Once men cease to believe in God, as G. K. Chesterton well said, it is not that they believe in nothing but that they believe in anything. Our civilised, educated, sophisticated age bears witness to this. Instead of God and angels, children today have spacemen and supermen. Dinosaurs and other miserable reptiles, real and fictitious, now call forth a child's wonder and admiration, whereas once the Creator and his works, the Saviour and his miracles, held sway over young minds.

Well has the apostle said: 'they changed the glory of the incorruptible God into an image made like to . . . creeping things' (*Rom.* 1:23). The results of all this atheism are to be seen in the numberless fears and superstitions that rack men's minds. When men pray to the creature and not to God they will find only an eyeless socket and not a gracious heavenly Father. It is the law of the moral universe that when men prefer not to fear God they will have to fear everything else.

The craving to be larger than life is something that we all feel at times. It is a temptation which besets us all our life. Man is such a poor, fallen, empty shadow of his once great original that he longs to inflate and enlarge himself into something more impressive than to be merely man. It was the folly of those kings and emperors of old who, like Nebuchadnezzar (*Dan.* 4) and Herod (*Acts* 12), aspired to be thought gods among men. It is the folly of many modern superstars and adulated sportsmen. The hand of sinners ever grasps for the shadow of greatness and importance.

The people of God must resist this carnal spirit. It is not of God but of the world. There should be no wish in a Christian, however gifted or important, to behave as if he were more than a mere man. This is one snare of the modern pulpit. It can so easily become a platform on which a preacher aims to strut with self-importance. Never was the danger of ministers grasping to become supermen greater, probably, than in the world of today, where electronics and amplification, spotlights and video cameras make self-aggrandisement so much easier than ever before.

It is so easy to read the Epistles of Paul and not to notice how consciously scrupulous he is always to be thought nothing more than a man. Towering gifts and sublime revelations from God might so easily have led him to grasp at the image of the superman. But he mortified this lust in every part of his ministry and in every line of his writings. He refused to adopt the Olympian style of the false prophet and spoke rather as a real man to real men. This is seen very clearly in his Epistles.

When Paul writes to the Roman Christians he begins by telling them that he longed to be 'comforted together' with them, as he says, 'by the mutual faith both of you and me' (*Rom.* 1:12). Seldom have such young Christians been so respectfully addressed by a visiting preacher of international renown! When he writes to the Corinthians he makes a very full display of his humanity. Not as a spiritual superman but emphatically as a genuine mortal, he tells them how he was with them at the first 'in weakness, and in fear, and in much trembling' (*1 Cor.* 2:3). So far is he from pretending to be larger than life that he declares: 'Let no man glory in men' (*1 Cor.* 3:21). The apostles, he affirms, are not supermen but only 'stewards of the mysteries of God' (*1 Cor.* 4:1). The believer must learn 'not to think of men above that which is written, that no one of you', as he says, 'be puffed up for one against another' (*1 Cor.* 4:6).

So far was Paul from wanting to put the apostles on a pedestal that he could write: 'I think that God hath set forth us the apostles last, as it were appointed to death: for we are made a spectacle unto the world, and to angels, and to men' (*1 Cor.* 4:9). Not only so, but these same apostles, though the greatest ministers of all history, were in their day 'made as the filth of the world' and as 'the offscouring of all things' (*1 Cor.* 4:13).

These expressions, and a score of others like them in Paul's Epistles, illustrate how determined he was to reject the image of the superstar and how insistent he was that none should have an exaggerated view of himself or the other apostles. What he exclaimed to the men of Lystra he virtually declared wherever he went: 'We also are men of like passions with you' (*Acts* 14:15).

It would have been well if ministers who followed the apostles in after years had adopted the same humble style of thought and speech. As it was, in the following centuries the ministry gradually became a sacred order whose importance was bolstered by ever growing claims to the possession of almost magical powers. In the course of time the Protestant Reformation recalled people to the good old apostolic attitude to preachers, that they are to be honoured as ministers of the Word of God and nothing more. But the danger of church leaders' reaching to be larger than life is an ever-present one, as the twentieth century itself still bears witness at times.

We do not wish to be misunderstood. Let every Christian and every preacher strive to the full to excel in every way. To be content with mediocrity when we might rise to a higher standard is a criminal wastage. Let every believer be the best he can with the gifts he has received. There is such a thing as excellence, and sometimes even superlative excellence. It is every believer's duty to be the best he can be and to do the most he can do for his great Master. To this end we need to stir up the gift of God within us, to attend to reading, praying and every other form of service to Jesus Christ. With such excellence no one can have any complaint.

The danger which we are here referring to is of using the gospel ministry to become 'lords over God's heritage' (*1 Pet.* 5:3). Such is the level of ignorance in some Christian circles that the preacher is allowed to become a guru and his claims as a leader are received with unthinking servility.

It is to protect the flock from such demigods that the Scriptures teach us to 'try the spirits' and to 'prove all things' (*1 John* 4:1; *1 Thess.* 5:21). When church leaders climb so close to heaven that they can claim to slay us in the Spirit, or fill us with the Spirit or make us drunk with the Spirit – and rumour has it that such super-ministers do exist – it is about time that Christian persons began to 'try' and to 'prove' these claims with a healthy scepticism. When preachers reach up to grasp for themselves the titles of 'prophet', 'priest' or 'apostle', it is surely high time for God's flock to study carefully the validity of their credentials. When scholars claim to be able to re-write the church's historic creeds and confessions and to transmit God's message to man more accurately through the medium of their own brains, rather than through the pages of holy Scripture, it is surely time for Christian congregations to watch their step.

It is a sign of spiritual immaturity when we are over-impressed with those who are larger than life. A safe rule is this: 'Beware the superman.' The super-loud talker, the larger-than-large self-styled leader, the preacher who 'guarantees' results, the man who brings his pedestal with him when he comes to the fellowship – these and all such men ought to put us at once on our guard by their very great eminence and importance.

The Apostle Paul has some pertinent things to say about persons of this kind. He speaks of church leaders in his own day who 'commended themselves' and who 'measured themselves by themselves and compared themselves among themselves' (*2 Cor.* 10:12). Evidently he had watched them and noticed their manner of operating in the churches. They 'stretched themselves beyond their measure' and were not above 'boasting of . . . other men's labours' (*2 Cor.* 10: 14–15).

He was forthright in the rebuke he gave to Christians who lusted after supermen-preachers: 'Ye suffer [it], if a man bring you into bondage, if a man devour you, if a man take of you, if a man exalt himself, if a man smite you on the face' (*2 Cor.* 11:20). Evidently Paul had a low opinion of supermen. He put it bluntly in these terms: '[A minister must not be] a novice, lest being lifted up with pride he fall into the condemnation of the devil' (*1 Tim.* 3:6).

We said earlier that there is in rational beings the appetite to be something higher and better than we now are. That need not surprise us. This life was not meant by God to be our final condition. Adam's paradise was intended at best to be a picture to him of a higher and better paradise above where man's every aspiration and wish would be finally and eternally satisfied. God made us for himself and we shall be fully happy as men only when we see God and are, in Christ, made fully blessed with him. That day is close at hand for all God's dear children. Soon – very soon – all believers will come to the highest pinnacle of all their hopes and desires. In heaven we shall be raised, in Christ, to the most perfect status and condition which we could ever wish or desire.

Our Saviour's lowly example, however, reminds us that the true way to mount up is not to grasp for honours but to humble ourselves, as he did, to be nothing in this world. After all, 'the last shall be first, and the first last' (*Matt.* 20:16).

Please, no more evangelical supermen.

30

Love of Truth and Its Opposite

To love truth is to love God, for God is truth. On the other hand, to set a low value on truth is to show contempt for God, whose truth it is.

To state that God is truth is to say that truth in all its forms is his property, that it has his approval and that he blesses all those who believe and affirm it. Everything in the Bible is truth. This refers not simply to the general message of the Bible or to its doctrines and teachings, but also to its historical statements and its judgements on men and on society.

The effect on us of reading and studying the Bible will be to fill us with respect for God's truth in all its forms. The worldview which the Bible teaches is intended by God to become *our* worldview. We are meant to be mentally, as well as spiritually, shaped and moulded by the Bible's view of everything. Its explanation of how the universe began, its interpretation of sin, death and eternity, its moral standards, its method of salvation by Christ, its 'three-storeyed' picture of heaven above, hell beneath and earth between – all these and all other aspects of the Bible's teachings are to fill our minds till they become our instinctive way of thinking and speaking.

The last thing we are commanded by God to do is to 'demythologise' the Bible, that is to look for an 'inner core' of truth from which we are to discard some outer rind of mythical unreality. The Bible is not written to be an enigma or a conundrum. It is truth for sinners that they may find salvation. When academic and scholarly men treat the Bible like a coded message which only the university professors can understand, they cast a slur on the goodness and wisdom of that God who gave us the Bible so that our souls might be fed with the truth.

To love the truth is an act of worship. Indeed, it is one of the highest acts of worship which we can offer to God. The non-Christian cannot love the truths of God's Word and, in fact, he cannot really love anything belonging to God. This seems too strong a statement to make at first sight. What about children who are well brought up in a Christian home? Do they not love the truths which they are taught in their parents' home before they come to Christ? They may appear to do. But when they come to years of maturity it is our sad experience to see that unconverted children have not really loved those truths which they appeared to have loved while they were still in their parents' care. When character is formed, the non-Christian shows his inability to love what God says.

The above-mentioned inability of the unconverted man to love God's truth is a fact which we must hold on to in our minds all our life. It explains important things to us and it keeps us from great anxiety in this life. The fact is that we meet and shall meet many in this life who are professional students of the Bible and yet who betray their lack of love for its teachings. We meet preachers and scholars who in their preaching and writing show that they do not love or believe what they have promised professionally to believe.

The same thing is true of some professing Christians who are in good churches. They are well brought up and well instructed, yet they betray the terrible fact that they treat God's truth cynically, coldly or without conviction of its importance. To love the truth is an act of the Christian's soul by which he perceives that what is in the Bible is from God, that it is precious and that it is to be asserted and defended in the Name of God. This love of truth is the same as conviction. It is an inner persuasion and certainty that what the Bible teaches is absolute truth.

Where Christians have this conviction of truth there will be unity and great strength. It is the mark of every great age of the church that believers have strong assurance of the truths of Scripture. They feel their vibrance and they are animated by their life. Men who have conviction of the truths of the Bible cannot help speaking 'often one with another' (*Mal.* 3:16) about them. Love of truth generates passion, zeal for God and a readiness, often, to die for the faith.

It can be upsetting and alarming to the inexperienced Christian to meet, either personally or in their writings, professional churchmen who do not love the truth. The tender mind and conscience of a true child of God is wounded by sermons or writings which are false to God's Word. Every Christian has had the experience of reading or hearing religious teachers who, professionally and intentionally, say things which would weaken their faith in God's infallible Word. It can put a stumbling block in front of the weak believer to do this. It can shake his confidence for a time. It can make him careless in his walk with God. 'Evil communications corrupt good manners' (*1 Cor.* 15:33).

The Christian must always keep in mind the sad fact that a church leader or Christian scholar, so called, may be a 'wolf in sheep's clothing' (*Matt.* 7:15). He may appear pious, gifted, learned, well-read and well-educated. But these qualifications, good as they are, do not prove that a professional churchman is a converted man. The evidence of being converted is that he preaches the truth, that he encourages his hearers to accept the Bible 'as newborn babes' (*1 Pet.* 2:2), that he says nothing irresponsible and nothing unscriptural. To *know* the truth is no proof of being a man of God. It is *love* of the truth that shows that he is called of God and sent by God to feed Christ's sheep.

There is a difference between lesser errors and greater ones. The term 'heresy' is to be used only of very serious errors. To deny the Trinity, the Godhood of Christ, the personality of the Holy Spirit, the sinfulness of mankind, the atoning character of the cross is to teach serious error. The term 'heresy' should be restricted to a denial of orthodox doctrine on such major points as these. It is not helpful to bandy the term 'heretic' about as if it could be used of any preacher who deviates in any degree from sound doctrine.

However, if we love the truth we must watch out not only for such major errors as the above but also for significant elements in a preacher's emphasis which betray that he may have a secret dislike of 'the whole counsel of God'. Preachers who have a secret agenda of their own to infiltrate their false ideas into churches seldom betray their intentions all at once. If they do, of course, they can be easily detected and brought to account. It is more probable by far that they will conceal their agenda and present the outward appearance of being orthodox while they stealthily drop their unsound ideas into men's minds in a diluted form.

Churches do not become unsound in one day. It is always by a process of slow liberalisation. First the orthodox and accepted teaching of a church is honoured with lip-service. Then it is devoutly questioned. At length it is declared to be open to objection. Finally it is rejected and abandoned outright. Those who cling to the orthodox teaching now become the victims of a character assassination. They are dubbed 'old-fashioned', 'traditionalists' and the like.

What lies at the root of all liberalisation of Christians and churches is lack of love for the truth. This is not difficult to understand. Truth is holy because God who is its Author is holy. Truth makes demands upon us. Truth has claims which go far beyond the intellect. It requires a life of obedience to God's revealed will. It demands that we 'walk in the light' (*1 John* 1:7). It is impossible to love truth and to love sin. Those who practise sin are morally incapacitated from loving truth. Good morals and sound convictions rise or fall together. History shows that it has always been so. The psychology and make-up of man guarantee that it will be so to the end of time.

Love of truth is not first and foremost a thing of the mind but of the heart. It is a by-product of grace and is an index of our sanctification. So long as grace reigns in the heart of the Christian and in the corporate life of the church, orthodox and biblical doctrine will remain in place. It will be welcomed and cherished for what it is.

However, once men grow cool in their attachment to the truth of God, the church enters into a very dangerous condition. Unsanctified intellects will sooner or later find an excuse for watering down the plain teachings of God's Word. This will at first be by speaking ungenerously about this or that unwanted item of their church's creed or confession. Men now talk of 'getting back to the Bible' and of 'getting away from human dogmas'. They speak of their creed as though it were in opposition to their Bible. To the unwary it sounds plausible. But it is in reality a sign of beginning to fall away from the truth. It is the first step to what, if unchecked, will be complete apostasy from the Christian faith in the end.

Those who love the truth and who are in sound churches must be on their guard at once when their public teachers begin to use expressions which reflect badly on their confessions of faith or articles of belief. It is the sure evidence of an inward dissatisfaction with sound doctrine. The listener may be certain that the public teacher in question has much more dissatisfaction with his church's creed than he is at present letting on. Given time, he will depart more and more from the path of orthodoxy.

This must be so because there is a *tendency* in both truth and error. Departure from truth at one point will, given time, tend to become departure at every point. A man's departure from his church's creed may seem very slight at first. But it will, if it is significant, move farther and farther away till it bears no resemblance to the original position in which his church stood. Once leave the path of truth and men (and churches too) will not stop till they have gone the whole way. The last stage is that their ultimate creed is the very *opposite* of all that they first professed.

If anyone doubts the accuracy of the above assertion, let him study the creeds of the Early Church and compare the early evangelicalism of these creeds with the later superstition and sacerdotalism of their medieval counterparts. Let those who think that we have gone too far in stating our case compare the Creeds and Confessions of the Reformed and Lutheran churches of the Reformation era with the *real* beliefs of many 'Reformed' and 'Lutheran' churches of this century. It is a true saying: 'Every institution becomes its opposite in time.'

The secret of loving truth is by keeping ourselves in the love of God. This is a profoundly practical and essential duty for every professing Christian. It is the duty of 'keeping the heart with all diligence' (*Prov.* 4:23). Once any generation of Christians begins to take truth for granted, it has moved on to the suicidal path. God, who reads men's hearts and motives, knows very well when his truth is thought to be irksome. He will probably give them time to repent. But if this is not done, he will assuredly remove their candlestick from them because they have 'left their first love' (*Rev.* 2:4). Not without reason does Paul warn us: 'They received not the love of the truth . . . And for this cause God shall send them strong delusion' (*2 Thess.* 2:10–11).

The sending of the delusion is the giving of men over by God to what will damn them. When truth is not loved, delusions sent as a judgement by God will be loved instead. Unloved truth takes wings and leaves men to delight in their lie, till they perish in it as a just recompense for their perversity. The lie may be evolutionary theory or modernism or deism or a score of other delusions. But it will take hold of those who cease to love truth till it consumes them and their church 'with the timbers thereof and the stones thereof' (*Zech.* 5:4).

Oh with what trembling should we adore God for giving us his holy Word! Oh with what affection should we study his truth every day we live! They are the best lovers of truth who bend every nerve to be obedient to God's revealed will in all its parts.

Did not Christ himself cry out: 'Lo, I come . . . I delight to do thy will, O my God: yea, thy law is within my heart' (*Psa.* 40:7–8). All who love truth say, Amen.

31

More Than a Dream

I was carried back in my dream to the olden days, and I was set down outside a church built of rough stone and surrounded by a graveyard. It was service time, for as I stood at the church door the simple people of that place were wending their way to the house of God, summoned by a bell. Old men and women, those in the prime of life and their children with them, walked quietly along in groups. Their modest dress and restrained conversation showed their respect for the Sabbath and betrayed the fact that they were preparing their minds for the worship of God before they entered the house of worship.

When the church was full I was taken in my dream inside and caused to sit unobserved in a seat near the front. No ornament disfigured the building. I saw no stained glass figures, no cross, no altar, no superstitious symbol. The wooden pews were neatly shaped, the walls bare, the ceiling rafters strong and rugged, like the worshippers themselves. A gallery at the back, like the ground floor, was filled with people silently waiting for the service to begin.

Suddenly the bell ceased and with scarcely a pause a side door opened and a group of venerable elders moved forward to take their places in the seat beneath the pulpit. Last of all came the minister. He was an old man dressed in black and with white hair. His back stooped a little and his walk was slow and uneven. The eyes of all were on him as he mounted the pulpit steps and opened the book from which God's praise was to be sung by all the congregation. As I looked at the old preacher I saw there was a mixture of sternness and gentleness written in the lines of his face. He opened the little book of spiritual songs with fingers which seemed as if they stroked each familiar page affectionately. I later saw that, when he came to read the large Book before him on the pulpit cushion, he turned each leaf with love, as a man might turn the pages of a volume made of gold.

When the selected song was announced and partly read over by the preacher, the congregation commenced singing the praises of the God who sits above upon his throne. At first it sounded like the voices of men. But as the sacred psalmody proceeded I was aware that a glory began to fill the house. In my dream I remember looking up as the singing died away and I saw what I am sure had not been there before – shining beings above the heads of the worshippers and, higher still, as if it were a great shadow of the very throne itself. When I saw this, I felt I knew not what of awe and calm reverence. I am sure that others felt it too because I noticed a change come over the people, especially the older ones, who no doubt had had experience of these things in the past. Several hid their faces in their hands. But even so I saw that they could not hide the tears in their eyes. It was a holy time.

Next, the preacher prayed. His words were not affected but plain, natural and full of scriptural thought. He addressed God as one who is accustomed to the work of conversing with the Eternal. Each measured sentence carried with it some lofty thought of the divine greatness, as if he would enjoy the very thought of God to the utmost of his power. Each subsequent petition craved a vast measure of grace, pardon and support for all his people. In my dream I glimpsed the fall of satanic powers as he prayed and I thought I saw in vision the dawning of that bright day when the church of Christ is all made up and the state of glory come in. His Amen was so solid and resounding that I thought the distant heavens above thundered with their echoing approval. The people's hearts too had been in that prayer for I perceived that not a few of them sat down with the beauty of holiness on their faces.

When the readings of the preacher from the great Book were finished and all the earlier singing concluded, I saw that he rose to preach his sermon and the people settled to listen to him as those who are about to hear a messenger from God. A solemn hush came upon all the congregation as he announced his text and proceeded to bring forth things old and new out of the Scriptures. I myself listened to the man's voice as earnestly as if he had been an angel, for he seemed to glow as he warmed to his theme. Indeed, his frail form grew strong again as he got into his subject and his hoary hairs shone about his dear head as he declared his Master's message. About half an hour into his sermon the preacher paused to look around him, especially on the young, and he had to draw out his handkerchief because his eyes were now streaming with tears of pity and fatherly love. I thought his heart would break at the thought that even one of his hearers might fail to meet him in the heavenly kingdom above.

It was at this point that I had my attention drawn to a young man seated not far from me. I had noticed him before because he seemed to be out of his element in that place. He wore a fine suit of clothes and obviously felt proud of his appearance. From time to time he had looked down at his watch like someone eager to be out of the sanctuary and back in the world. I had seen him out of the corner of my eye with pity. But I had not paid any very special attention to him till now, when the preacher started to weep over the souls of those who were careless. Then a wondrous change came over the youth. As when a spark from the blacksmith's forge flies out at random and catches alight in a heap of dry straw, so some sentence of the preacher's must have burned into his young heart with mysterious power. In an instant the youth's countenance was altered. He was riveted by the preacher. He forgot himself and all this world. Instead he saw himself dangling over a lake of everlasting fire and felt the first dreadful gnawings of the worm which will forever devour the consciences of the godless in another world.

When the sermon was over this youth lifted up his head from his knees. For all the rest of the time since the change began in him, he had it hidden as low as it could go. When I saw it again it appeared to me to be the face of a new man. I never in all my life saw a more chastened expression on any man and I knew that he had felt the peace which all those feel who abide under the shadow of the throne.

The service being ended with a benediction, the venerable preacher came slowly down from his pulpit and the elders rose in respect and each man grasped his hand before he left to return to his room. And so the people quietly went out, some with a heavenly shine on their faces, and some with their heads bowed low for fear of grieving the majestic Being whose house they had been privileged to sit in.

As for me, I did not know whether I had been out of the body or in the body. But my heart burned in me as I rose, all unnoticed, to go out after them all. I tried, as I left, to discover what church this had been where I had so sat and worshipped. But it was more than I could do to find this out. I supposed though that it might have been in some Puritan place years ago, or in New England amongst its early pilgrims. Or was it in the Wales that once was . . . or in some Scottish glen? I partly think it did not matter where I was on earth because it had been a meeting with eternal things. I recall that when I got outside, the sky was blue and the sun was hot above me. And when I thought of God I wept aloud for very happiness.

Now I had this dream some time ago and I had not expected to tell it to any man, but I tell it now because I recently had the dream all over again, as I must now explain.

In my second dream I stood outside the church I saw before. It was a Sabbath and there came along the street, now finely paved and very broad, that same young man whose spiritual alteration I have told about. But now the youth was grown old and slow. He walked with difficulty on a stick and in his face there was some similarity to the venerable preacher through whose sermon he had come to love heavenly things. At the church gate he stopped and drew out a key to enter the building where his fathers once worshipped God. There were no crowds to fill the house of prayer any more. Neglect and poverty could be seen on every hand. To tell the truth, he was the only man alive who would take any care of the place where once great worship had been offered up. But wars and human fickleness had changed society since his youth. Death had carried his forefathers to the grave. Alone this aged saint would every week open the house of worship for love of God and man.

In my dream I followed the man inside and heard him sigh as he looked on every hand and muttered 'Ichabod' as if to those who had once been fellow worshippers with him then. Not twenty persons gathered for the service that was held in that place once in the month and which happened to fall on this day. As for me, I was caused to sit where I had sat in my first dream and it was so very different I could have wept till my eyes were dim. But as I waited for the service to begin I saw a young man, light and trivial, walk up the pulpit steps and his face bore a foolish smile which contrasted incongruously with the face of the old preacher whom I had seen in my earlier dream. No shining beings came in with us as we sang, nor did we sense the shadow of the throne above us as we listened to this new kind of sermon making. For all that I can remember, there was little else in the sermon other than dull comments and a few unprepared remarks which raised a momentary laugh. A few did laugh, especially of the most ignorant persons present. But I observed that such laughter only produced a painful look on the old elder's face. But this he hid as best he could. He hoped the best of all, and clearly thought that he should not appear uncheerful to the young who, he said often to himself, have never known the glories of past days. After the service was over I saw that the old saint spoke kindly to every one, especially to the children. Much to my surprise and pleasure, I saw that he did not speak severely to the novice preacher but took from his inside pocket a volume of choice theology, which he asked the young man kindly to receive as a gift and urged upon him the importance of secret prayer.

There being no one else to close up the building but the old man, he waited till the little gathering of people had all gone and then, with as much care as if it were a palace, he checked every door and finally locked the stout iron gate. He did not, as I expected, make straight for home but picked his way through the old gravestones till he came to the monument which marked the place where his own beloved minister had been laid to rest many years ago. Here he took off his hat and laid his stick against the stone. With difficulty he got down upon his knees, and I saw that he must have done this often because the grass of that spot was worn down with his constant kneeling in prayer. Above his head the sky was blue and the sun shone down warm and bright.

I wish it were permitted to me to tell you all that I heard and all that I felt as the old saint poured out his prayer to the Eternal, for I heard every word in my dream but I may not repeat it all now. But so much I may tell. When this man lifted up his soul I heard him groaning to the God of his fathers. One phrase he repeated as if his dear heart would crack: 'Return, return, return, O how long?' He wrestled in his praying as if with an angel. Indeed, I verily believed an angel would appear, so loudly did he cry out and so deeply did he groan.

His praying done, the old man rose unsteadily to his feet and reached for his stick and for his hat so as to go home. And as he turned to go I heard and saw a thing which, I am certain, he was not aware of. But I, being in my dream, both saw and heard it clearly. In the distant heavens came the gentle roll of thunder and on the far horizon appeared again the presence of the shining beings I had seen in my first dream. Then – awesome to relate – across all that land appeared the shadow of the throne of him who lives forever and who answers prayer.

Whether the old man knew it or not I cannot say, but I saw that there would be a new morning for that church, so long neglected and decayed. Even as I looked to the far horizon I saw a glimpse of the glory which was to come in God's wise time.

And when I awoke I knew it was more than a dream.